Christmas in

UKRAINE

Christmas in UKRAINE

Christmas Around the World From World Book

World Book, Inc.
a Scott Fetzer company

CHICAGO

Staff

Publisher Emeritus
William H. Nault

President
Robert C. Martin

Vice President, Publisher
Michael Ross

Editorial

Managing Editor
Maureen Mostyn Liebenson

Associate Editor
Karen Zack Ingebretsen

Writer
Ellen Hughes

Permissions Editor
Janet T. Peterson

Art

Executive Director
Roberta Dimmer

Art Director
Wilma Stevens

Senior Designer
Brenda B. Tropinski

Senior Photographs Editor
Sandra Dyrlund

Photographs Editor
Feldman & Associates

World Book, Inc.
233 N. Michigan Ave.
Chicago, Illinois 60601
http://www.worldbook.com

For information on sales to schools and libraries, call 1-800-975-3250.

Printed in Singapore
3 4 5 6 7 8 9 10 01

Product Production

Director of Manufacturing/Pre-Press
Sandra Van den Broucke

Vice President, Production and Technology
Daniel N. Bach

Manufacturing Manager
Barbara Podczerwinski

Senior Production Manager
Randi Park

Proofreaders
Anne Dillon
Carol Seymour

Direct Marketing

Director, Product Development
Paul Kobasa

World Book wishes to thank the following individuals for their contributions to **Christmas in Ukraine**:
Family of Michael Burdiak, Eugene and Sophia Daczyszyn, Marta Daczyszyn-Ulane, Stephanie Daczyszyn and Nicholas Zook, Iwanna T. Gorchynsky, Maria Harasowska-Daczyszyn, Ulana Hrynewych, Michael Jula, Olha Kalymon, N&M Design, Solomea Pavlychko, Elaine L. Rook, Katie Sharp, Family of Victor and Christina Taran, the Ukrainian National Museum (Chicago, Illinois), and Christina Ulane.

Library of Congress Cataloging-in-Publication Data
Christmas in Ukraine.
     p. cm.—(Christmas around the world from World Book)
Summary: Describes the celebration of Christmas in Ukraine; includes sections on native songs, recipes, and fun-to-do crafts appropriate to the holiday.
     ISBN 0-7166-0897-9 (hc)
     1. Christmas—Ukraine—Juvenile literature. 2. Ukraine—Social life and customs—Juvenile literature. [1. Christmas—Ukraine. 2. Ukraine—Social life and customs. 3. Holidays. 4. Christmas decorations. 5. Handicraft.] I. World Book, Inc. II. Series.
GT4987.55.C49 1997
394.2663'09477—dc21   97-22522

CONTENTS

THE UKRAINIAN PEOPLE

The history of Ukraine is a story of greatness and oppression. It is of a strong, deeply religious people; a people who have kept their culture and traditions alive through centuries of struggle, not only in their homeland but across the world. Wherever Ukrainian communities thrive and prosper, magnificent church architecture and unique folk art reveal the story and character of these resilient, faithful people.

At Christmas, the true nature of the Ukrainian people is evident. Their willingness to work hard and their generosity, which are basic to the Ukrainian character, are lovingly handed down from generation to generation around the Christmas table. In their many religious rites and age-old traditions of Christmas, Ukrainians pay tribute to the sources of their strength: a deeply held faith, love of family, and a sense of oneness with nature.

Stretching from the Carpathian Mountains on the west to Russia on the east, and from the Prypiat Marshes on the north to the Black Sea on the south, Ukraine is the second largest country in Europe. It is a country rich in natural resources, which is the country's blessing—and its curse.

The word *Ukraine* means "borderland," which offers a clue to its curse. Since this country's beginning, people fortunate enough to inhabit this fertile land have seen their country overtaken time and again by neighboring countries envious of their wealth.

Ukrainians are a Slavic people with their own distinct language and culture. Through centuries of oppression, three periods of independence stand out: the Kievan-Rus period, from the 800's through the 1300's; the Kozak period, from the mid-1500's to the late 1700's; and 1917-1920, the period between control by czarist Russia and the Soviet Union. Today, Ukraine is free once again and struggling to rise above economic woes accumulated during years of Soviet rule.

Of nature and family

Since the earliest time, tribes of Ukrainian peoples inhabited this abundant realm with its fertile fields and its rivers teeming with fish. Living in close harmony with the land, early Ukrainians had a deep understanding of the power of nature. They felt a close connection to the animals and plants around them. They believed that everything, from the animals they hunted to the fields that bore their crops, had a soul that could be appealed to and must be respected.

These early Ukrainians worshiped the forces of nature—the sun, fire, thunder, rain, wind, and frost. They recognized the power of each to affect their lives for good or bad. Among their many gods were *Perun*, the god of thunder; *Dazhboh*, god of the sun; and *Veles*, god of domestic animals. Many Ukrainian rituals and tradi-

the agricultural cycle of planting, harvesting, and storing crops. At the same time, every festival was a ritual commemoration of the family, both past and present. Christmas in Ukraine today retains a strong connection to the feast days of this ancient winter cycle.

Celebrating earth's cycle

Like people everywhere, the ancient Ukrainians celebrated the winter solstice and its promise of the return of the sun and longer, warmer days. The Ukrainians' ancestors told and retold a lovely myth to explain the earth's cycle of changes:

Lada, the sun princess, loved Iur, the lord of thunder and rain, and they were married. Together they blessed mankind and the earth with eternal spring and multiplying love.

The dragon, Koshchii, ruler of autumn, arrived and caused the trees to change to their mourning colors of crimson and gold. Maryna, the Grandmother and Sorcerer of Winter, joined forces with Koshchii. Together these two villains wove a plot to kill Iur and kidnap Lada, imprisoning her in an ice castle. Here, Lada's warming smile faded.

Koshchii and Maryna then set about destroying mankind. Trees were stripped naked and the rivers and lakes turned to stone. Birds flew away and animals lay asleep as if dead. Men hid in their huts covered by a white shroud of snow.

Fortunately, Schedryk, deity of the moon, came to man's rescue. Taking the form of a silver-haired wolf, he sprinkled the dead body of Iur with the water of life, hidden in the snowy shroud. The once lifeless Iur rose like a thunderbolt

Ukraine is the second largest country in Europe. Only Russia is bigger. Ukraine lies in southeastern Europe and borders seven other countries and the Black Sea. The country's coat of arms *(top left)* features a design that dates from the late 900's.

tions of today have their roots in rituals once performed to please these ancient gods.

Also central to the lives of Ukrainians of yesterday and today is the religion of clan, or family. For early Ukrainians, everything in life centered on the family. All members of the clan—the living, the dead, and the yet to be born— were thought to exist on earth together. In particular, the spirits of the departed were thought to be present in daily life. All generations of the family—past, present, and future—were welcomed home to celebrate feast days.

The ancient Ukrainian calendar of festivals was connected to

and rode the wolf to rescue Lada. As they journeyed back to earth, Lada expelled Maryna with a smile.

Reunited, Lada and Iur danced in joy on earth. Everywhere the lovers' feet touched, the icy shroud melted, revealing the earth's rich bounty beneath. Once again, the earth was restored to life and abundance.

Ancient Ukrainian peoples worshiped the sun god and celebrated his return at the winter solstice. The agricultural cycle, which is naturally aligned with the changing position of the sun, is the central focus of many age-old Ukrainian religious traditions. The spring, summer, fall, and winter cycles of ritual traditions and feast days all correspond to the work cycle of planting, early harvest, final harvest, and preparation for the next growing cycle.

Work, play, and worship are all tightly interwoven in the daily life of Ukrainians. Religious observance is not a break from everyday life but instead an important part of life.

Christmas comes to Ukraine

"...we knew not whether we were in heaven or on earth.... Their service is fairer than the ceremonies of other nations. For we cannot forget this beauty."

—from the report of Prince Volodymyr's emissaries to Constantinople, having observed the Byzantine Rite of the Orthodox Church.

Ukraine's vast, open plains are covered with fertile black soil, which has made this country one of the world's leading farming regions. About one-third of Ukraine's population lives in rural areas.

An ancient manuscript tells the story of how Prince Volodymyr of Kiev brought Christianity to Ukraine and its people.

During its greatest period of independence—the Kievan Rus era—Ukraine became a world-class power and a center of culture. Ukraine's capital city, Kiev, earned its lasting reputation as the Mother City of Rus. Also, Christianity came to Ukraine.

In 987, Prince Volodymyr of Kiev sent representatives to visit other capitals and observe the great religions of the world. After reading the report of his emissaries to Constantinople, the prince himself quickly left to see the world with his own eyes.

In 988, Prince Volodymyr re-turned to his country a Christian and set about to likewise convert his countrymen. Destroying the idols to the gods of nature that had stood on a hill near his palace, Volodymyr built St. Basil's Church in their place.

The citizens of Kiev were ordered to the Dnieper River, where they were conducted through mass baptisms and initiated into their new state religion. Christianity spread throughout the countryside and, encountering only a few pockets of resistance, the ornately beautiful Byzantine Rites of the Orthodox Church found acceptance in the hearts of the Ukrainian people.

For the Ukrainians, becoming Christian did not mean abandoning all their agrarian beliefs and traditions, however. Instead, these people blended the old and the new, giving fresh meaning to existing rituals.

Worship of the sun god was replaced with a love for the Son of God, as ancient gods of nature faded into forces controlled by the Christian God. The religion of the family, or clan, with its focus on the living spirits of ancestors blended naturally with the Christian concept of heaven. For Ukrainians, faith is a deeply satisfying Christianity, which makes room for centuries of Ukrainian tradition.

Over time, the Ukrainian winter cycle feast known as *Koliada* was transformed into a beautiful, family-centered celebration of Christmas as new Christian meanings were layered onto age-old traditions.

Free again

In 1988, as they stood at the birth of a new, independent Ukraine, Ukrainians celebrated the 1,000th anniversary of the arrival of Christianity to Ukraine. With their new-found freedom, the people of Ukraine looked forward to the rebirth of public religious ceremony throughout their country.

The oppression and hardships of the 1900's have been some of the most difficult for the Ukrainian people, and their religion, to bear. In World War II (1939-1945) alone, about 5 million Ukrainian civilians were killed.

This painting, entitled *Millennium of Christianity in Ukraine,* commemorates the arrival of Christianity to Ukraine. Taking place in 1988, this anniversary came on the heels of new-found religious and social freedom for Ukrainians living in their homeland.

When the country fell under Soviet rule, a concerted effort was made to break the strong cultural ties that unite Ukraine's people. When Stalin came into power, he set about wiping out the Ukrainian national identity, religion, and even the Ukrainians themselves. During Soviet occupation, Ukraine's natural resources were mismanaged and plundered and the country's skies, rivers, and land polluted.

The grand churches of Ukraine were silenced during this time—torn down, shuttered, or converted into movie theaters, discos, and warehouses. Hundreds of other churches, from majestic cathedrals in the capital to graceful little village churches were razed.

During more than 70 years of Soviet oppression in Eastern Ukraine and more than 40 years in Western Ukraine, when the entire country was made a Soviet state, generations of Ukrainians grew up without the benefit of their culture's religious beliefs and traditions. Publicly celebrating Christmas, Easter, and other essential rites of the church was forbidden for many years.

. . . Christmas lived on in the hearts— and secretly in the homes—of many Ukrainians.

As private religious practices were forbidden, Soviet state celebrations were offered in their place. Russia's Grandfather Frost (*Died Moroz*) and a non-Christian celebration on New Year's Day were offered as a replacement for Ukraine's beloved St. Nicholas and the rich tradition of Christmas in Ukraine.

Still, Christmas lived on in the hearts—and secretly in the homes—of many Ukrainians. Miraculously, a number of grand religious structures, such as the Caves Monastery and St. Sophia's Cathedral in Kiev, remained intact. With the rebirth of Ukraine, these awe-inspiring treasures have been restored to their original purposes and have been reborn to the service of God.

Today, Kiev, once "the golden city of 400 churches" is alive with spirit again. In cities across Ukraine, the centuries-old tradition of Orthodox ritual and the heart-satisfying sound of Ukrainian choral music fill the sanctuary. In homes where Christianity and the ancient religions of family and nature had been absent for decades, the old ways are being learned anew.

The majority of Ukrainians adhere to the Orthodox faith. There is a large Ukrainian Catholic Church and smaller religious communities of Jewish, Baptist, Evangelical, and Muslim worshipers.

The country's history of oppression and conflict has naturally led to the creation of two separate Orthodox churches: the Ukrainian Orthodox Church and the Ukrainian Autocephalous Orthodox Church.

The Ukrainian Orthodox Church, formerly the Russian Orthodox Church, was the only sanctioned church during the years of Soviet domination. This church is still connected to the Moscow Patriarchate. The Ukrainian Autocephalous Church has the same service, but gives its allegiance to the Ukrainian Patriarchate in Kiev. The Ukrainian Catholic Church, also called the "Uniate Church," which was created by a "union" between the Catholic and Orthodox churches in the 1500's, also follows Orthodox ritual, but is aligned with the Pope and the Roman Catholic Church.

The Ukrainian diaspora

The Ukrainian celebration of Christmas is close at hand in many places outside Ukraine today. In fact, some traditions lost to Ukrainians under decades of Soviet oppression may now be found only in the homes of the Ukrainian diaspora, communities of Ukrainians that are scattered outside the homeland and across the world.

In addition to the many who live in territories just outside the borders of their former country, approximately 5 million Ukrainians now reside in Europe, North and South America, and Australia. The largest Ukrainian communities outside Ukraine are in Canada and the United States.

In every place they have settled, Ukrainians have built strong, successful communities. And at the heart of every Ukrainian community in America and Canada stand impressive Orthodox and Catholic churches in testimony to the importance of faith in the Ukrainians' daily lives.

The oppression of Ukrainian religion and culture plus the call of new opportunities abroad have driven several major waves of Ukrainian emigration since the

1870's. Leaving Ukraine, these immigrants carried with them their deep-felt religious faith and ancient family traditions.

Though a few Ukrainians ventured to the New World in time to participate in the American Revolutionary War, the first and largest wave of immigration of Ukrainians to the United States and Canada came between 1870 and World War I (1914-1918). More than 600,000 Ukrainians made their way to the mining and industrial centers of the northeastern United States or to the fertile central plains of Canada, where they put their farming expertise to use.

Today, millions of Ukrainians live outside the homeland, spreading the unique characteristics and Christmas traditions of their culture around the world.

The Beauty of Ukrainian Churches

MANY CHURCHES IN UKRAINE, INCLUDING SOME OF THE FINEST RELIGIOUS ARCHITECTURE IN THE WORLD, WERE PURPOSEFULLY DESTROYED DURING THE DECADES OF SOVIET DOMINATION. THOSE THAT WERE SPARED, INCLUDING ST. SOPHIA CATHEDRAL, KIEV'S OLDEST STANDING CHURCH (BUILT IN 1037), ARE WONDERFUL EXAMPLES OF THE MAGNIFICENCE POSSIBLE WHEN DEEP FAITH AND HUMAN EFFORT ARE JOINED.

THE CAVES MONASTERY IS ABOUT 2 MILES SOUTH OF KIEV. WITH ITS FASCINATING GOLD-DOMED CHURCHES, UNDERGROUND LABYRINTHS CONTAINING MUMMIFIED MONKS, AND LOVELY MONASTIC STRUCTURES, IT WAS THE KIEVAN RUS'S FIRST AND MOST FAMOUS MONASTERY. TODAY, IT CONTINUES TO BE ONE OF KIEV'S MOST ENTRANCING TOURIST ATTRACTIONS.

UKRAINIAN IMMIGRANTS AROUND THE WORLD HAVE BUILT IMPRESSIVE CHURCHES, WHICH STAND AT THE CENTER OF THEIR COMMUNITIES AND

THEIR LIVES. FOR EXAMPLE, THERE IS WINNIPEG, CANADA'S SS. VLADIMIR AND OLGA CATHEDRAL AND PITTSBURGH'S ST. JOHN THE BAPTIST UKRAINIAN CATHOLIC CHURCH.

SOME OF THE MOST BEAUTIFUL CHURCH ARCHITECTURE IN UKRAINE IS ALSO THE SMALLEST AND MOST REMOTE. TRADITIONAL UKRAINIAN WOODEN CHURCHES TUCKED AWAY IN TINY VILLAGES ARE ELEGANT WORKS OF ART. NOT A SINGLE NAIL IS USED IN THEIR CONSTRUCTION. RATHER, THE BEAMS ARE CAREFULLY SHAPED AND PLACED TO FIT TOGETHER IN PRECISE HARMONY.

A UKRAINIAN CHURCH SERVICE IS COMPOSED MORE OF SINGING THAN RECITING. TO THE WORSHIPERS, SINGING IS CONSIDERED MORE LIKE PRAYING. THERE IS NO MUSICAL INSTRUMENT. ONLY *A CAPPELLA* SINGING IS HEARD, SO THE SOUND OF GOD'S OWN INSTRUMENT—THE HUMAN VOICE—WILL NOT BE DIMINISHED BY INFERIOR ACCOMPANIMENT.

Beautiful gold-domed churches tower over the Caves Monastery, just outside of Ukraine's capital city of Kiev (left). Scattered throughout the country, the smaller wooden churches of Ukraine are in and of themselves some of the most beautiful works of art Ukraine has to offer *(above)*.

Sharing faith

Having left just before Ukraine came under Soviet domination, these early immigrants were able to transport a full, rich celebration of their religion and

As in their homeland, Ukrainians in the United States celebrate Christmas with rich tradition. Shown here are the sacred icons of Mary, Jesus, and St. Nicholas as they are displayed during a Ukrainian-American celebration of Christmas.

its rituals to their new land. As two more waves of immigrants followed them, between the two World Wars and after World War II, these "first-generation" immigrants were able to help the newcomers recover the religious traditions that had been taken from them.

Together these generations of Ukrainian immigrants built centers of Ukrainian culture and tradition around the world. Today, in close-knit Ukrainian communities in New York, Chicago, Pittsburgh, and Cleveland, in the Canadian provinces of Alberta, Manitoba, and Saskatchewan, and in every place Ukrainians came to stay, the sounds, sights, and tastes of age-

old Ukrainian traditions abound at Christmastime.

With characteristic hospitality, American and Canadian Ukrainians continue to welcome new immigrants to the familiar warmth of their communities. Over the years, Ukrainian community-based organizations have been formed by a self-reliant people determined to provide for the immigrants' every need.

As it did in the homeland, religion stands at the center of life in these Ukrainian communities. Ukrainian churches play a major role in organizing religious, cultural, and community events. Ukrainian schools everywhere invite the world around them to their annual St. Nicholas Day celebrations. Ukrainian national museums and cultural centers in New York, Chicago, and Toronto preserve and promote their religious and cultural traditions for all to witness. At the Ukrainian Cultural Heritage Village near Edmonton, Alberta, and the University of Pittsburgh's Ukrainian Nationality Classroom, the specifics of Ukrainian architecture, art, culture, and daily life are presented in loving detail.

The ties between Ukrainians and their homeland remain ever strong. There is a brisk business in sending food, gifts, and necessities to the old country. And there is a never-ending demand for flights home to visit. News of Ukraine and its economic and political struggles are of utmost interest to Ukrainians everywhere.

Today, as people in Eastern Ukraine struggle to reclaim a faith suppressed for more than 70 years, Ukrainians in the United States and Canada reach out to offer support and to help reintroduce long-forgotten Christmas traditions.

Ukrainian folk art

Over the centuries, the Ukrainians' rich spirituality and close communion with nature have found creative expression in many different art forms. Like other aspects of the culture, Ukrainian folk art is treasured around the world for its unique beauty and design.

Designs in art vary from region to region across Ukraine, but a similarity of basic pattern and use of symbols unites Ukrainian artistic expression. Geometric patterns have been a constant theme since 2500 B.C. Later, symbols representing plants, animals, and the forces of nature also became traditional.

Ukrainian folk art uses a variety of art forms, including wood carving, metalwork, weaving and tapestry, embroidery, beadwork, ceramics, and *pysanky* (Easter egg decoration).

Wood carving. Familiar around the world as intricately carved boxes, beads, candlesticks, and bracelets, Ukrainian wood carving developed into a fine art in the creation of church design. Carved iconostases, lecterns, columns, and crosses grace Ukrainian churches everywhere. The wood carvings of the Hutsul region are lavishly encrusted with mother-of-pearl, various shades of wood, colored beads, brass wires, and metal plaques.

Metalwork. Lavish Ukrainian metalwork also

Ukrainian wood carvings, with their intricate design and awe-inspiring beauty, are known around the world.

can be viewed in cathedrals, where extravagantly worked gold, silver, or tin frames encase sacred icons. Gorgeously designed jewel-encrusted crosses, chalices, and other religious artifacts in gold and other precious metals evidence the devoted effort of Ukrainian artists.

Weaving and tapestry. Practical and beautiful, Ukrainian weaving is a truly an ancient art form. While the Oriental and southern European influences can be noted in some early weaving, Ukrainians soon brought their own special style of composition and coloration to the creation of *kylyms* (rugs), cloths, kerchiefs, and aprons.

Embroidery. Embroidery is the most commonly practiced folk art in Ukraine. The complexity of stitches and the wealth of colors have taken basic cloth decoration to a higher aesthetic level. Subtle differences in design can be easily observed by comparing *rushnyky*, or ritual cloths, from various regions of Ukraine.

Beadwork. Similar to Ukrainian embroidery in its complexity and striking use of color, beadwork ranges from simple decoration to the creation of extravagant collars and necklaces. Geometric patterns and figures worked into Ukrainian beadwork bear a striking resemblance to the work of Native Americans. Less common today than embroidery, Ukrainian beadwork also displays interesting regional variations.

Ceramics. Ukraine's prehistoric inhabitants dug into the land's deposits of high-quality clay to produce ceramic goods.

The delicate stitchwork and colorful designs of Ukrainian embroidery are characteristic of this unique folk art. Embroidery is the most commonly practiced folk art in Ukraine—and no one does it better.

Over time and under the influence of Byzantium, early primitive patterns of design were replaced by rich ornamental motifs. Other styles—Gothic, Renaissance, and Baroque—were adopted gradually and added to the richness and variety that enlivens this regional craft. Today, Ukrainian ceramic design incorporates geometric patterns along with plant, animal, and bird representations.

Pysanky. Ukrainian-decorated Easter eggs are prized the world around for their complex beauty. Covering the tiny, curved surface of an egg, delicate designs present the patterns and symbols echoed across all forms of Ukrainian art.

Each region of Ukraine is known for its own form of pysanka art. The Hutsul people of the Carpathian Mountains create highly geometric designs, while in Eastern Ukraine, egg decoration focuses on floral design. Symbols on the eggs present the oldest religious traditions, including the sun, eternity, the forces of nature, and animals, along with Christian symbols such as crosses and churches.

From ancient time, pysanky were thought to possess magical powers, providing protection from evil, thunder, or fire. Then and now, pysanky are given as a sign of friendship and a wish for health. As part of the Easter ritual, pysanky are blessed at the church.

The patterns of design used to decorate Ukrainian ceramics have changed over the years. Today geometric patterns and plant, animal, and bird representations define this colorful art form *(above and left)*. The folk art that truly defines Ukraine just may be the *pysanky,* or Ukrainian-decorated Easter eggs *(shown above)*. Today they are given as a sign of friendship and a wish for health.

THE DAYS BEFORE CHRISTMAS

Christmas in Ukraine overflows with meaningful rituals and traditions. It combines a deeply religious observance of the birth of Christ with ancient agrarian winter-cycle rituals and festivals.

Officially, the Christmas season spans the days from the Feast of the Presentation, December 4, to the Feast of Jordan, January 19. This holiday calendar coincides with the ancient winter-cycle celebration of Koliada, a time of thanks for the sun god's return.

Before the days of Christmas feasting and celebration comes a 39-day meatless, milkless Advent fast and a busy period of preparation. Following age-old ritual, everyone rolls up his or her sleeves for plenty of plain hard work. Everything—harvest, home, and heart—must be in perfect order for Christmas.

All field work, harvesting the fall's crops or preparing for the coming year, must be finished before December 4, the Feast of the Presentation. This feast day, which celebrates the presentation of Mary as a child at the temple, marks the beginning of Advent. Families must now focus on making everything in their lives ready for the arrival of the baby Jesus. To this end, there is no work in the fields from this day until the winter holiday cycle comes to an end.

The house, the barn, and everything on the property must be fixed up, finished, and made like new. Cottages, always kept in tidy order, are to be carefully repaired, if needed, and freshly whitewashed inside and out. Every speck of dust must be swept away, while taking special care not to disturb any spider webs—a good-luck charm, especially at Christmastime. A new ritual cloth, or *rushnyk*, is lovingly embroidered and draped about the family icon, where it will rest when not in use in important ritual observances throughout the season.

The barn, too, must get a thorough going-over. The building is repaired, and every harness, every farm tool put in good working order.

Financial affairs also must be "mended." All debts should be paid or forgiven, all financial promises kept, and financial records brought up-to-date.

Most important of all is the preparation of the spirit. Before a heart can welcome the baby Jesus, torn friendships must be mended, arguments settled and forgiven. Following ancient rules, while a person may take action to protect himself or herself from evil spells at any time, no words may be spoken in anger on the holy days of Christmas.

During this season of winter-cycle rituals and Christmas preparation and celebration, marriage is forbidden, as are dancing and merrymaking of any kind.

Magic of the Spider

Though the house is to be cleaned from top to bottom and every speck of dust swept away, any spider web discovered at Christmastime must be left undisturbed throughout the holidays. Spiders and their webs are symbols of good luck that can be found everywhere at Christmastime in Ukraine. They come in the form of Christmas tree ornaments, decorations, or the real thing—if you're lucky. The spider is considered a most Christmasy creature to Ukrainian children, who grow up hearing stories of the spider's legendary Christmas kindness.

According to one popular story, a young widow was sad at Christmas because she had a tree but no money to buy presents for her children or decorations for the tree. As the family slept on Christmas Eve, a spider took pity and wove a magical web on the tree. In the morning, the mother and her delighted children woke to find their little tree covered with a beautiful, glittering, silver web.

In another story, a spider is credited with giving the Christ Child His first plaything. As the baby Jesus slept that night in the manger, a stable spider wove an intricate web above him in the rafters. When baby Jesus woke, the light of dawn made the early morning dew sparkle on the delicate web. The baby smiled and laughed at the beautiful sight.

As Christmas Day draws near, energy is focused on the work that must be done for the special day itself. After all, no work may take place on the holy holiday. Plenty of wood must be chopped and stacked to fuel the stove for cooking and heating. Then there is the cooking and baking for the feasting to come. All foods that can be prepared in advance are readied.

The traditions of Christmas preparation that are important to modern-day Ukrainians can be traced back directly to pre-Christian, winter-cycle holiday rituals.

According to tradition, Ukrainians see no separation between work and worship. Feeding the animals, tending the fields, baking bread—all the everyday activities of life—are filled with meaning and can be performed as acts of worship. In preparing for Christmas, the bonds between man and nature and between work and worship seem to touch every moment of the day. As they make their hearts and homes ready, modern-day Ukrainians around the world feel the deep pull of clan and nature as ancient rituals bring about strong feelings.

Draped in beauty

A rushnyk is a hand-embroidered towel or cloth used in religious rituals in the home. The direct translation, "towel," is misleading, because the rushnyk is a near-sacred object that, when used, confers great honor or respect.

All work on the fields must be complete by December 4, the Feast of the Presentation, as Ukrainian families must now focus their efforts on preparing for the celebration of the arrival of the baby Jesus.

An icon of Mary carrying the baby Jesus is lovingly draped with a hand-embroidered rushnyk.

meal, is carried in a rushnyk by the *hospodar*, or head of the household. When greeting guests to her home during the holidays, a *hoshodynia*, or hostess, holds an offering of bread and salt in her rushnyk-draped hands. Children take food from the Sviata Vecheria meal and other treats wrapped in the safety of a rushnyk to their grandparents and godparents.

In working the design into the borders of her family's rushnyk, a woman follows the colors and pattern preordained by generations of tradition. The embroidered borders display intricate geometric patterns and other ancient symbols of eternity and the clan, reinforcing the Ukrainians' deep connection to their spiritual past.

Rushnyky stand as a symbol for the eternal life of the family. All generations come together, and so the ritual cloth is present at every important passage in life. At rest, the rushnyk is draped about one of the family icons in a holy place of honor in the home. This sacred towel is an essential part of every meaningful ceremony. A newborn baby is wrapped in a rushnyk, a rushnyk is bound around the new couple's joined hands at marriage, and a rushnyk is wrapped about the body to prepare it for burial.

A new rushnyk is lovingly embroidered as part of the traditional preparation for Christmas. Then it is draped about one of the family icons to await the celebration. The *kutia*, an important dish of the Sviata Vecheria, or Christmas Eve

The feast days of Christmas

While there is plenty of work to be done, the Advent season in Ukraine is also a time of celebration. The weeks of preparation before Christmas are enlivened with special Christian holy days and rituals rooted in the past.

The Feast of the Presentation (December 4). This celebration of the presentation of young Mary at the temple opens the Advent season. This day also officially ends the autumn season of agricultural work.

In the past, all sorts of protective rites were employed on this day to ensure fortune in the coming year. "Blessed" water from streams where three waters meet was used to fend off illness and evil and to make love potions. Cows were sprinkled with seeds, their udders buttered and enveloped in smoke so they would give lots of milk. The smoke was thought to protect the cows from the spells of evil forces. Cows were also fed a thick, sour soup to ensure that their cream would be thick.

St. Catherine's Day (December 7). While weddings are forbidden until after the Christmas holidays, wedding wishes are often in the air during the season.

On the eve of St. Catherine's Day, young men fast so that God will give them a good wife. Following tradition, a young girl cuts a branch from a cherry tree and places it in a bottle of water in-side the house. If the branch sprouts flowers before *Malanka*, or New Year's Eve, it will bring her luck in the coming year. Young unmarried girls tell fortunes this day and share a communal supper. With a pot of borscht (beet soup) and one of *kasha* (groats) from the meal, the girls take turns climbing onto the gate outside and "inviting fate to supper."

The Day of the Apostle Andrew (December 13). Officially commemorating the apostle who spread the Gospel to Eastern European countries, including Ukraine, this is a day of merry amusement for unmarried young men and women. Following age-old tradition, young women tell fortunes with little cakes and

The Ukrainian belief that work and worship are one is most apparent in the preparation of the church for the holy celebration of Christmas. Here a woman carefully sweeps the floor of her church.

Today, many Ukrainian communities around the world, especially through their local church, have a Saint Nicholas Day (December 19) celebration. This continuance of an old tradition may help Ukrainian children remember that before Santa Claus there was a holy man named Nicholas.

melting wax, listen for dogs' barking, ask passersby their names, and summon their "beloved" to appear in a dream—all in the hopes of learning the identity of their future husbands. Young men pass the day playing pranks on neighbors and teasing the girls. The day ends with a game in which boys and girls try to take bites from a cake that hangs from the ceiling.

St. Barbara's Day (December 17). Honoring an early martyr of the church, this day signals to all Ukrainians that the coldest days of winter are coming quickly. To Ukrainian children, however, this day signals that the fun of St. Nicholas Day is only two days away.

St. Nicholas Day (December 19). In the hearts of Ukrainians everywhere, St. Nicholas—*Sviatyj Mykolaj*—follows only Jesus and Mary as an adored spiritual guide. Icons of his kind and gentle visage can be found in the most sacred spot in nearly every Ukrainian home. Churches and schools are named for him throughout Ukraine and wherever Ukrainians have settled around the world.

St. Nicholas's special hold on the Ukrainian heart may be attributed to the influence of Prince Volodymyr, who brought back sto-

A Tale of Two Calendars

CHRISTMAS DAY IN UKRAINE, AND IN UKRAINIAN COMMUNITIES AROUND THE WORLD, FALLS ON JANUARY 7, IN ACCORDANCE WITH THE JULIAN CALENDAR. THE NEWER GREGORIAN CALENDAR, ADOPTED BY THE ROMAN CATHOLIC CHURCH IN 1592, BECAME THE STANDARD FOR MOST OF THE WORLD. HOWEVER, THE UKRAINIAN CHURCHES NEVER MADE THE SWITCH AND STILL MARK RELIGIOUS DATES BY THE OLDER JULIAN CALENDAR.

IT IS NOT THAT THE CELEBRATION OF CHRISTMAS FALLS ON A DIFFERENT DAY, BUT INSTEAD, THAT THE DAY COMES LATER ON THE JULIAN CALENDAR. ALL AGREE THAT DECEMBER 25 IS THE DAY TO CELEBRATE CHRIST'S BIRTH. THE DIFFERENCE HAS TO DO WITH WHEN THIS DATE ARRIVES.

HERE IS A COMPARISON OF SPECIAL CHRISTMAS HOLIDAY DATES AS OBSERVED FOLLOWING THE JULIAN AND THE GREGORIAN CALENDARS.

	GREGORIAN CALENDAR	JULIAN CALENDAR
FEAST OF THE PRESENTATION	NOV. 21	DEC. 4
ST. NICHOLAS DAY	DEC. 6	DEC. 19
SVIATA VECHERIA (CHRISTMAS EVE)	DEC. 24	JAN. 6
RIZDVO (CHRISTMAS DAY)	DEC. 25	JAN. 7
ST. BASIL'S DAY	JAN. 1	JAN. 14
JORDAN (EPIPHANY)	JAN. 6	JAN. 19

ries about the kindly bishop when he brought Christianity to Ukraine.

Born in A.D. 280, in Asia Minor, St. Nicholas, who came to be the Archbishop of Myra, led a life of deep religious faith and legendary kindness. Today he is considered the patron saint of children and sailors.

As little children, Ukrainians learn from their parents the many stories and legends of St. Nicholas and his wonderful wisdom, courage, and kindness. There are the stories of how he secretly supplied dowry money to three poor sisters so that they could marry, how he saved sailors time and again from disaster at sea, how he fed the starving people of Myra, and how he refused to renounce his faith though exiled and imprisoned. It is even said that a magical oil flows from the crypt that contains St. Nicholas's remains.

As little children, Ukrainians learn from their parents the many stories and legends of St. Nicholas.

In honor of the bishop's legendary kindness and generosity, St. Nicholas Day is an occasion for merry celebration for Ukrainians.

On the eve of St. Nicholas Day, little children set plates on the windowsill—or in some regions, set their shoes by the hearth—in hopes of receiving a gift and a treat or two from the kindly bishop. Then, before hurrying the little ones off to bed, the whole family joins in singing a special carol in honor of St. Nicholas.

Later that night, St. Nicholas is said to travel in the company of several little angels who assist him in his secret work of bringing happiness to Ukrainian children. Should he encounter any youngsters on his way, he is likely to quiz them about their religious education. Traveling with him is a "chort," a rascally character who looks out for naughty children. Not so nice himself, the chort is likely to leave a switch or two on the pillows of children in need of correction.

The windowsill is the place to look for surprises in the morning. This is because when St. Nicholas gave dowry money to the three poor maidens, he is said to have tossed it through their window. In honor of St. Nicholas's role as a secret benefactor, many Ukrainians sneak to the doors of friends, neighbors, or those in need on this special night to anonymously leave "St. Nicholas presents."

On St. Nicholas Day, each child wakes to find treats of candy and fruit on his or her plate, along with special presents—traditionally, three: one to wear, one to play with, and one to wonder over.

Family members also may exchange gifts this morning. These gifts are often accompanied by clever poems or notes describing the gift receiver in a playful way or making a wish for that person in the coming year. The poems, composed by family members for each other, are more important to the celebration than the gifts themselves. Whatever else they may or may not receive, each family member is given at least one new item of clothing to wear in the coming year.

St. Nicholas Day is traditionally a festive day filled with visiting among friends, neighbors, and family in every Ukrainian community.

In the United States and Canada, schools and community groups present St. Nicholas Day pageants and parties. Children sing and perform, there is plenty of Christmas fare to enjoy, and St. Nick himself, dressed in his lovely bishop's robes, arrives bringing gifts for all.

St. Nicholas holds a permanent place in the hearts of Ukrainians because he was a real person, a religious figure who set a powerful example with his kindness and generosity.

Immaculate Conception of the Blessed Virgin Mary (December 22). This is the final holy day before Christmas. Believing that, while Mary was conceived like any other child, she was born free of original sin, Ukrainians and other Christians in the Eastern Orthodox Church have celebrated this holy day since Christianity first came to Ukraine. In the 1800's, this feast day became an official tradition of Catholic churches around the world.

Ukrainian icons

Icons hang at the heart of every Christian Ukrainian home. Icons are the most sacred object of the Christian faith in Ukraine.

A Ukrainian woman lights a candle in celebration of the Immaculate Conception of the Blessed Virgin Mary on December 22.

Sacred paintings of Jesus, Mary, St. Nicholas, or other revered saints, these icons can always be found in a home's most holy place, usually on an eastern wall of the dining room, near the "altar" of the family table. Here, family members pray while gazing into an icon's image. The family's rushnyky are draped respectfully about the home's icons when not in use. The *didukh*, a sheaf of wheat that houses the spirits of the family during the Christmas season, is placed here, under the holy protection of the icons.

To understand the power and beauty of an icon, you must first understand that it is not simply a religious painting. In fact, icons are not to be judged by traditional standards at all but according to their unique purpose. The paintings seem dark and, until you understand their meaning, inaccessible. The images appear austere, abstract, overly somber. The poses of Mary, Jesus, and the saints seem stilted; the figures are sometimes out of proportion to each other, their expressions incongruous.

Icons are said to be "written," not painted. They are considered to be the words of the Bible brought to life. Icons may be written in paint on wood or plaster, in stone or tile mosaics, or in enamel on metal. They are intended to present reality in the heavenly realm, not the world as we know it here on earth. Every proportion, every expression symbolizes some aspect of that heavenly truth. In an icon of the nativity scene, for example, Mary

An icon of St. Nicholas shows this kindly bishop in his traditional pose: his right hand raised in blessing and his left hand clutching the Gospel.

is always presented as a much larger figure than those around her because of her greater importance. Joseph is small and placed off to the side in accordance with his lesser role.

The stable pictured on an icon is a dark cave, symbolizing the darkness of the world in sin before Christ brought His light. It also symbolizes the cave where Christ's body was laid after the crucifixion and before He rose from the dead. Above, the star shines out brightly, symbolizing the light Christ brought to banish the darkness. The baby's swaddling clothes also represent the shroud in which Christ's body later was wrapped.

Animals are always in the center of things in a nativity icon, reminding the viewer that the animals were the first to welcome the baby Jesus. They also symbolize all of nature, which was changed by Christ's coming. Other figures—shepherds, wise men, angels—may vary from one nativity icon to another. Some people not actually present at the birth, such as John the Baptist, may be added to the scene because of their important role in Jesus's life on earth.

An icon of Mary and the baby Jesus or of St. Nicholas presents the saints in predetermined poses first written hundreds of years ago. Iconographers may reveal their own individual style only in the pigment, texture of the background, or other such nonessential details.

St. Nicholas is traditionally

Sacred icons of Mary, Jesus, St. Nicholas, and other revered saints grace the walls of Kiev's St. Sophia Cathedral. The cathedral, built in 1037, is the city's oldest standing church.

depicted with his right hand raised in blessing and his left hand holding the Gospel, reflecting the Ukrainian view of the bishop as shepherd of the flock, defender of the faith, and intercessor before Christ.

From childhood, Ukrainians are taught to look at icons deeply and with respect in order to understand religious truths. While Ukrainians honor their icons by bowing before them or kissing them, this reverence should not be mistaken for worship, which is restricted to God and Christ.

In Ukrainian churches, the congregation is surrounded by icons. Most church icons are priceless objects, hundreds of years old. Yet some church icons, written in the same style, depicting the same poses and expressions, are new. Today, dedicated iconographers in the United States and Canada as well as in Ukraine keep this important religious art tradition alive.

SVIATA VECHERIA AND RIZDVO

At last, it is time to celebrate the birth of Jesus Christ. After all, He is what the Christmas season is all about. This part of the holiday begins the day before Christmas, the day that will culminate with Sviata Vecheria, Holy Supper. Sviata Vecheria is the most sacred and meaningful celebration of the Christmas season. The entire family—past, present, and future—will gather together tonight for this most important traditional supper filled with meaningful Christian and ancient agrarian symbolism. And the celebration will continue through the following day.

Everything about Sviata Vecheria—the gathering, the setting, and the meal—is layered with meaning. Symbols originally based in the ancient religion of family and the worship of the forces of nature took on added meaning when Christianity, and Christmas, came to Ukraine. All of these meanings now come together in the Ukrainian heart on this night of rich celebration and remembrance.

Specific customs vary greatly from village to village and across Ukraine. In addition, many modern Ukrainians have had to alter their traditions to fit an urban lifestyle. Still, Ukrainians around the world continue to hold dear the rich traditions and underlying meanings of Sviata Vecheria. And they still actively embrace many of the age-old rituals.

Viliia (*Veleeya*), beginning at sunset the night before Christmas Eve and extending through Christmas Eve day, is a time of intense preparation for Sviata Vecheria. All family members are expected to stay together in the *hospodarstvo*,

or family home. Also, there should be peace at home now. Any argument could lead to misfortune in the year ahead.

In the cozy, well-scrubbed cottages of a traditional Ukrainian village, Sviata Vecheria preparation begins with the lighting of a new fire in the *pich*, or ceramic-tiled oven. Ancient ritual requires that each log be individually blessed as it is placed into this fire. Water used is also specially blessed.

With the first rays of sun on the morning of Christmas Eve, every door in the house is thrown open to receive *pravedne sontse*, or the blessing of the sun. Now it is time for the hospodar to go to the barn. He must ensure that the animals are well cared for and well fed.

Next, the didukh, which is a symbolic sheaf of wheat that will house the spirits of the clan throughout the Christmas celebrations, is brought in the house and placed in a position of honor near the family icons and the Sviata Vecheria table. This sacred spot is

Late in the day, the *hospodar* (head of the household) officially begins the celebration of Sviata Vecheria as he presents the didukh with great honor and ceremony. The didukh is a sheaf of fine grain thought to house the spirits of the family for Christmas.

to the house by the hospodar and his oldest son.

In some regions, the didukh is simply pulled together and tied with a rope; elsewhere it is bound with a chain. In one part of Ukraine, the stalks are woven into ornate braids and flowers and tied with blue and yellow ribbons. In modern urban homes and apartments, the didukh may be represented simply by a few stalks of wheat in a vase. Regardless of its size or ornamentation, the didukh stands as a strong central symbol of faith and tradition in Ukrainian homes everywhere.

When the didukh is in its place of honor, time is magically transformed. Normal time is suspended; no work can be done while the didukh and its spirits reside with the family. All efforts must focus on the rituals of celebration. Now the spirits are truly believed to be residing with the family and taking part in the holiday celebration. And here they remain until the Feast of Jordan. At the ceremonial close of the winter cycle of holidays, the didukh is taken to a field, spread out in the shape of a cross, and burned to free the spirits.

On the morning of Christmas Eve, the meatless, milkless fast observed throughout Advent changes to an absolute fast. In abstaining from food throughout Christmas Eve day, Ukrainians remind themselves of the hardships endured by Mary as she traveled to the stable in Bethlehem.

Fasting is not difficult now. On this busy day, the family bare-

often the eastern corner of the room, the first place to receive the light of the sun each day

A home for spirits

The didukh (from *did*, meaning "grandfather" and *dukh*, meaning "breath," "spirit," or "ghost") is a ceremonial sheaf made from wheat and other grains from the fields. It is believed to house the spirits of family members, both the deceased and the yet-to-be-born, during the winter cycle of celebration.

In anticipation of Christmas, the hospodar gathers a selection of the best stalks from all his fields during *obzhynky*, the fall harvest. The wheat, rye, buckwheat, and other grains are tied into a sheaf and stored in the barn. At sunset before Sviata Vecheria, the didukh is ceremoniously brought

ly has time to think about eating. The stepped-up preparation for Sviata Vecheria and for Christmas itself now consumes nearly every moment. Still, Ukrainians know the wait and the labor will be well rewarded, for tonight is Sviata Vecheria, and a delicious 12-dish meal is being prepared for the celebration.

Preparing the table

In the Ukrainian home, the table where the family gathers to share its meals is considered an altar, a sacred place of celebration. As such, it must be carefully prepared for this most holy meal.

According to ancient tradition, tonight's table, as it is prepared for this meal of thanksgiving for the harvest, also represents the earth and prayer for plenty in the year to come.

First, a thin layer of hay is spread on the table and sown with seeds from each of the family's fields. In accordance with the old ways, fresh hay is scattered throughout the house, and the children are encouraged to roll in it and make animal sounds to bring health and safety to the farm animals in the new year.

A plain linen tablecloth is spread over the thin layer of hay, gently covering the earth, the dead buried there, and the fertile fields with a blanket of snow. Traditionally, this is the tablecloth where the family spirits will eat. Cloves of garlic now are placed on

All the preparations, both spiritual and physical, of the season have been leading up to this Holy Night. This final day of Advent is a day of anticipation; there is much to do before the special supper of the evening–Sviata Vecheria–can take place. Here, a young Ukrainian girl carefully prepares the table for Sviata Vecheria, making sure that everything–including the cloves of garlic to ward off evil–is safely in its place.

The Animals at Christmas

UKRAINIANS' LOVE OF FAMILY INCLUDES ALL CREATURES AND IS EXPRESSED IN THE LOVING CARE OF FARM ANIMALS AND PETS. LIVING CLOSE TO THE LAND AND IN HARMONY WITH NATURE, UKRAINIANS HAVE ALWAYS UNDERSTOOD THE IMPORTANT ROLE FARM ANIMALS PLAY IN THEIR PROSPERITY. WITH THE INTRODUCTION OF CHRISTMAS, UKRAINIANS WERE GIVEN EVEN MORE REASON TO PAMPER THEIR ANIMALS. AFTER ALL, IT WAS THE ANIMALS OF THE STABLE WHO SHARED THEIR HOME WITH MARY AND JOSEPH AND WHO WERE THE FIRST TO GREET THE NEWBORN BABY JESUS. AT CHRISTMAS, UKRAINIANS' LEGENDARY GENTLENESS AND GENEROSITY TOWARD ANIMALS TAKES ON RITUAL FORM.

EARLY IN THE MORNING ON CHRISTMAS EVE, THE HOSPODAR BEGINS HIS ROUNDS WITH THE ANIMALS. CAREFUL ATTENTION IS PAID TO THE ANIMALS' COMFORT AND HAPPINESS FOR THIS NIGHT OF ALL NIGHTS. ACCORDING TO THE ANCIENT RELIGION, VELES (THE GOD OF DOMESTIC ANIMALS) WILL VISIT THEM TONIGHT. GIVEN A MAGICAL ABILITY TO SPEAK ON THIS NIGHT, THE ANIMALS WILL TELL ALL WHEN VELES ASKS HOW THEY HAVE BEEN TREATED DURING THE YEAR. NEXT YEAR'S HARVEST MAY BE AFFECTED FOR GOOD OR BAD BY WHAT VELES LEARNS FROM THE ANIMALS.

IN THE HOUR BEFORE SVIATA VECHERIA, THE

HOSPODAR RETURNS TO THE BARN. LAYING HIS AX AT THE BARN'S THRESHOLD, HE LEADS THE ANIMALS ONE BY ONE OVER TO THE AX TO DRIVE AWAY ANY EVIL SPIRITS CLINGING TO THEIR FUR OR FEET. AS A FURTHER PROTECTION FROM HARM IN THE YEAR AHEAD, HE GIVES THEM ALL PURIFIED WATER TO DRINK.

FINALLY, TO MAKE THEIR VALUED ANIMALS TRULY A PART OF THE FAMILY CELEBRATION, A SAMPLING FROM EVERY DISH FROM THE SVIATA VECHERIA TABLE IS MIXED IN WITH THEIR FOOD AND SERVED TO THE ANIMALS .

Ukrainians consider their animals part of the family all the year around; but at Christmas, their love of animals takes on ritual form. After all, the animals shared their place of shelter with the Holy Family and gave up their manger for the newborn Christ to sleep in.

Traditionally, Sviata Vecheria was intended to offer in thanksgiving a taste of everything grown in the fields and garden of the hospodarstvo, or household, as the family asks for a plentiful harvest in the year to come. Rich with tradition and the fruits of the harvest, today it is both a thanksgiving and a celebration of the coming of the Christ child.

each of the four corners of the table to ward off evil.

Next, a second tablecloth is laid over the first, preparing the table for the living. This cloth is often one beautifully adorned with traditional embroidery. Three kolaches, the circular braided breads of Christmas, are next stacked in the center of the table. A beeswax candle is placed in the hole at the top of the stack, and evergreen sprigs encircle the bottom as decoration. The kolaches, which originally represented the eternal life of the family and the interwoven forces of nature, now also stand for the Christian Trinity. The bread's shape symbolizes eternity, the everlasting generations of the family together, and eternal life through Christ. The beeswax candle represents the hard work of the bees, which are seen as being like man in their labors, and it also represents the fruits of that labor. Lit, the candle symbolizes the light of the sun god and the star of Bethlehem or the light of Christ in the world.

After the ritual "first-course" *kutia* is served, a small bowl of this sacred grain and honey dish is tucked near the candle in the hollow at the top of the kolaches. Through this gesture, the kutia is symbolically offered to the spirits residing there.

The legs of the table are tied with string to ensure that the fruit trees on the property will grow straight and not break in the wind.

The floor under the table also is strewn with a fine layer of new hay, and small ax heads or other representational farm tools are placed in the hay to be blessed against rust or damage in the coming year. At the same time, treats for the children are hidden in the hay to be discovered after supper.

In a window, a glowing candle sends out a welcoming light to any lonely, hungry person who may pass by. Remembering the plight of Mary and Joseph on the first Christmas Eve, Ukrainian families want to be sure the light of their hospitality shines bright to any and all this night. Some Ukrainian families switch on every light from attic to basement and add candles all around to shine out their welcome bright and clear.

Everyone in the family must be present for Sviata Vecheria. If anyone fails to come or arrives late, it is said that someone will be taken from the family that year. A place is set at the table for anyone in the family who has died in the past year, so that he or she may join the feast. As they take their places, each person blows

Following the busy growing and harvesting season, winter with its cold and quietness has long been a time to retreat to the warmth of the home. In Ukrainian homes, this time, with the central religious holy days of Christmas, also has been a time for the family to come together, even when they might be separated by many miles.

on his or her chair to avoid sitting on any spirit who may be there.

An extra place is set to welcome any stranger or person in need who may come to the door. If a friend should come to fill that place, another empty place is set at the table, keeping the welcoming offer open.

As sundown approaches, the young children are stationed at a window to watch the skies. Sviata Vecheria will begin as soon as a child sees the first star of the evening.

Sviata Vecheria begins

With the Sviata Vecheria meal on the table and the family assembled, the hospodar throws open the door to call out the traditional welcome to the forces of nature and the spirit world.

"Most holy sun, most generous moon, bright stars, and lovely rains. Come to our house to eat Sviata Vecheria, to eat kutia. Holy spirits of our grandfathers, our great grandfathers, our fathers and our mothers, our brothers and our sisters, our children, our grandchildren, and our great-grandchildren. All souls come to our home to take part in the holy supper."

All must be welcomed tonight, so now a second call goes out, this one to the forces of evil:

"Evil frost, wild wind, burning rays of the sun, evil thunderstorms, all evil and bad things, come to our table to eat kutia."

When that invitation is not immediately accepted, it is happily canceled:

"I call you, but you are not coming. In that case, let me not see you near my house for a whole year to come. Reside then in the rocks, in snowbanks, in frost, in mountain peaks, in dark forests, in deep ravines, in cliffs, in the ice, wherever the voice of the rooster doesn't reach, and don't come back."

Now the family joins in prayer, not with bowed head but standing and looking up to heaven. Then, with the singing of the very first koliadky, or Christmas carol, of the season, the much-anticipated celebration begins.

Our daily bread

Ukraine, with its incredibly fertile, dark soil, its mild climate, and its long growing season, has at various times in its history been called the "Breadbasket of Europe" and the "Breadbasket of the Soviet Union."

Ukrainians have always appreciated the blessings that come from working this rich land. The country's flag of wide horizontal blue and yellow stripes calls up a picture of fair blue skies above abundant golden fields of grain. It was only natural for Ukrainians to have made bread, the product of their land and their labor, a deeply meaningful symbol of religion and ritual.

Bread has always been a most sacred food to Ukrainians. In a Ukrainian cottage, no bit of bread is ever wasted. A scrap dropped to the floor is kissed in blessing and tossed into the fire. The last crumbs from a loaf of bread are used to thicken soup, browned and buttered to garnish vegetables, or tossed to feed the birds. Regarding bread as a holy food and following the ancient belief that fire is also holy, a Ukrainian wife would make the sign of the cross over freshly shaped loaves and give thanks for her blessings as she placed them into the oven to bake.

In times past, Ukrainian villagers greeted honored guests at the door of their cottages holding

Ukrainians have always considered bread a sacred food. At Christmastime this is evident, as the rich-tasting kolach graces the Sviata Vecheria table. Circular in shape, kolach represents the family, eternity, prosperity, a rich and full life, good luck, and well-being.

•41•

out a loaf of bread topped with a mound of salt. This offering was meant to demonstrate genuine welcome and a willingness to share any and all the cottage contained. This bread offering is now presented only at church and official functions.

Ukrainians seem to have a special bread for every holiday and celebration. The *paska*, specially made for Easter when it is taken to the church to be blessed, is rich, round, and decorated with fancy dough ornaments and a cross. Then, there is the tall and tasty *baba* or *babka* ("grandma"), a rich cake bread baked for Easter, but hard to resist any time of year. The wonderful wedding *koroway* is a statuesque, intricately designed, and delicate-seeming tree made of bread and hung with symbolic dough ornaments.

The Sviata Vecheria meal traditionally consists of twelve dishes prepared in commemoration of the twelve apostles. While the dishes vary from region to region, all contain no meat or dairy products, as this still is a day of abstinence. Shown below are kutia, holubsti, varenyky, and pears in uzvar.

And at Christmas, there is the rich-tasting kolach. Its name derived from *kolo*, the Ukrainian word for "circle," the braided, circular kolach represents the family, eternity, prosperity, a rich and full life, good luck, and well-being.

Food of the gods

It wouldn't be Christmas in Ukraine without kutia. This "food of the gods" is the first course, and the one indispensable dish, of Sviata Vecheria. Kutia, a rich mixture of boiled wheat (sometimes barley), poppy seeds, and honey was first stirred up during a winter-cycle celebration over 5,000 years ago. It is served only during the Christmas holidays—first on Christmas Eve at Sviata Vecheria, then during Shchedryi Vechir, the grand meal of Epiphany Eve, the night before the Feast of Jordan.

Thousands of years before Christmas came to Ukraine, kutia was a symbolic dish prepared during the winter cycle of holidays. It may have originated as a symbol of the united family—past, present, and future generations. More likely, it was prepared as an offering to the sun god, presenting the best of the harvest in thanks and as a wish for plenty in the year to come.

Symbolically, the wheat stands for prosperity, the poppy seeds for the beauty of the land, and the honey for hope that the family will stick together.

The recipe for kutia varies from region to region, as does its ritual use and when it is served in

Ukrainian Christmas Eve Invocation

Sacred Sun; Benevolent Moon,
Bright stars, abundant rain,
Come join us for the Holy Feast—
to eat Kutia!

Our Holy grandfathers—forefathers,
Fathers, mothers, brothers, sisters,
Children, grandchildren—great-grandchildren
To all the spirits in our hearts—Lada
Come and feast with us!

Spiteful Frost,
Tempestuous winds,
Scorching rays,
Wicked storms,
Fierce and Bad—
Come and eat Kutia!

I call you! You do not come!
For all eternity you will not come!
So we may not disclose your identity,
To listen, they did not...

Petrified in rocks,
Steep-sloped, dark forests,
High mountains, deep precipices,
In snow—ice.

All spirits of our origin,
Come with us to eat Kutia!
Here's to God, King of Heaven.
To all deceased,
Reign in Heaven.

For us Luck, Health, and Long Life.

the meal. Served first as a ritual opening to the meal or last as a dessert, kutia is presented with great respect. In some regions, a new, never-used pot is selected for cooking the kutia. Before being served, the kutia is placed near the family icons and the didukh, in a position of honor.

When kutia is presented at the beginning of the Sviata Vecheria celebration, the hospodar walks around the table, carrying the bowl nestled in a rushnyk. He shares a taste of kutia with each person, moving from oldest to youngest, and exchanges the ritual Christmas greeting.

After everyone has been served, the hospodar calls out, "God gave heaven to all the dead to live in, and to us, luck, health, and good life," then he tosses a hardy spoonful of kutia to the ceiling. The bigger the mess on the ceiling, the better, according to Ukrainian tradition. The number of poppy seeds that sticks to the ceiling predicts how many healthy animals, productive beehives, and chicken eggs the hospodar can look forward to in the new year.

At the end of the meal, children take some kutia to their grandparents and godparents. And a serving of kutia is left on the table for the spirits of deceased family members, now residing in the didukh.

As the celebration of Christmas was joined to the winter cycle

> **The hospodar calls out, "God gave heaven to all the dead to live in, and to us, luck, health, and good life."**

festival more than 1,000 years ago, a legend about the origin of kutia helped to smooth the coupling.

In their flight to Egypt to escape Herod's search for the newborn king of the Israelites, it is said that Joseph, Mary, and the baby Jesus passed a farmer sowing wheat in his freshly plowed field. Later that day, soldiers arrived to ask the same farmer if he had seen fugitives on the road. The farmer honestly replied that a family had passed by when he was sowing his wheat. Looking at the field of wheat, which had somehow grown from seeds to harvest-ready maturity in one day, the soldiers assumed many days had passed since the family had walked by, and they gave up their chase. The miracle of the field of wheat saved the baby Jesus and added a new Christian significance to kutia.

Sviata Vecheria continues

The meatless, milkless fast of Advent continues right through Sviata Vecheria. Yet the meal manages to be a wonderful, multi-coursed celebration of the abundance God has provided. Traditionally, Sviata Vecheria was intended to offer in thanksgiving a taste of everything grown in the fields and gardens of the hospodarstvo, as the family asked for a plentiful harvest in the year to come.

After the ritual offering of kutia comes the toast to the dead, a strong shot of *horilka* (liquor), often flavored with strawberries, cherries, or caraway seeds. Everyone in the family must join in this often very emotional toast, pausing for a mo-

ment to pay tribute to family members who are no longer living.

In many homes, it is also customary for the head of the family to take bread from the table, dip it in honey, and serve it to each family member with a piece of garlic. By eating the honey and garlic together, participants show God that they will be thankful for anything given to them—the sweet and the bitter.

In all, there may be anywhere from seven to seventeen dishes served tonight, although the traditional number is twelve. The twelve courses originally stood for the twelve full moons in the yearly agricultural cycle and later came to represent the twelve apostles.

The traditional menu varies from region to region and from home to home, but it is bound to include appetizers of pickled herring, mushrooms, dill pickles, and borscht; boiled, baked, or jellied fish dishes; sauerkraut and potato dishes; *holubsti* (stuffed cabbage) with rice or buckwheat filling; beans, peas, and other vegetables; *pyrohy* (boiled dumplings) with fruit stuffings; *uzvar*, the sweet, traditional "drink of the gods"; and, in some regions, *knysh*, a ritual bread eaten in remembrance of the dead. Last comes the fruit *varenyky*, a rich, sweet dessert of stewed fruit. Each person must sample some of every dish served or risk refusing the bounty that God has provided.

This traditional family celebration is likely to last for hours, and it always ends with the joyful

This young Ukrainian boy is eager to begin the Sviata Vecheria meal, for he is looking forward to the end of the dinner, when he can scramble through the hay under the table in search of the treats and candy hidden there.

singing of favorite koliadky around the table. Meanwhile, the children happily scramble through the hay under the table to find treats and candy hidden there. Gifts may be exchanged, and the hospodar may give money to each of his children.

When the meal is finished, the children take food to the homes of their grandparents and godparents. By doing so, they symbolically include them in the family circle of celebration.

Now, *Sviata Nich*, or Holy Night, has begun. Food is left on the table for the spirits to enjoy. The beeswax candle on the kolach is left to burn itself out. If the smoke of the candle rises straight, a good year is forecast; if it drifts, a bad omen is feared.

Invited to Sviata Vecheria, the spirits of the family are welcomed to stay in the home throughout the holiday season. This night, other spirits also are said to roam. Every person keeps unpleasant or angry thoughts out of his or her mind to keep evil spirits away. Traditionally, the hospodar and older members of the house keep an all-night vigil to guard the house from harm.

At midnight or early the next morning, everyone but the sick or very old attends a Christmas Mass. The service is filled with beautiful choral music. In some places, the Christmas Mass begins at midnight and continues until the first light of Christmas morning.

Rizdvo–Christmas Day

Calling a merry "*Khrystos Rozhdaietsia!*" ("Christ is born!") and answering "*Slavite Yoho!*" ("Let us glorify Him!") into the starry night, families head home from Midnight Mass to prepare for a merry

Christmas Day of caroling and visiting with family, neighbors, and friends.

The 39-day fast ended with Midnight Mass, and the delicious, long-forbidden holiday meat dishes and rich, creamy pastry delights await carolers and friends at every home. There will be traditional *medivnyk*, Christmas honey cake; *medivnychky*, honey cookies and bars with fruits and nuts; poppy seed tortes; crisp dainties; filled crescents; and more.

Celebrating the birth of Jesus, Rizdvo also ushers in the ancient winter-cycle celebration of Koliada. In its ancient form, Koliada combined fall and spring agrarian traditions in a joyful celebration of the return of the sun. Koliada also was thought of as a spirit capable of influencing the harvest. In the past, Ukrainians talked about "calling the Koliada" to join in the Christmas season celebration and "shooing away the Koliada" when the winter cycle ended.

In modern times, Koliada, which spans the week between Christmas Eve and New Year's Day, is a time of feasting, singing, fortune-telling, and gift-giving.

Christmas Day also begins a three-day celebration in the Orthodox church. The celebration continues the next day with the Synaxis of the Blessed Virgin Mary, a feast day celebrating Mary and Joseph as the newborn Christ's guardians on earth, and ends with the Feast of St. Stephen, a celebration of the first Christian martyr.

Christmas Day marks the beginning of a three-day celebration in the Orthodox church, during which time a series of masses is offered. After Christmas is a feast day celebrating Mary and Joseph as Christ's guardians on earth, and the Feast of St. Stephen follows on December 27. Here a mass is celebrated at St. Volodymyr Cathedral in Kiev.

GENEROUS EVE

Shchedryi Vechir or "Generous Eve," also called Malanka, is the spirited Ukrainian celebration of New Year's Eve. In some regions, Malanka is held on the eve of the Feast of St. Basil (January 14). In other places, the New Year's Eve celebration doesn't occur until the eve of the Feast of Jordan (January 19). No matter when it arrives, Malanka is a night for fun.

The Feast of Jordan commemorates the baptism of Christ in the River Jordan by John the Baptist. This feast day officially closes the Ukrainian winter cycle of celebration. One of the most important religious events of the year, it is filled with religious ritual and customs.

"Generous Eve" is a fitting description of the feast held to herald the arrival of a new year. Like Sviata Vecheria, this evening's feast begins with the presentation of kutia, the essential and most holy part of the meal. Here again, a number of dishes will follow, though the number may vary this time.

Unlike Sviata Vecheria, Shchedryi Vechir is a truly sumptuous feast. Free from the restrictions of the pre-Christmas fast, this meal is an out-and-out delight, featuring delicious meat dishes and rich pastries sure to satisfy. Some traditional foods include baked pyrohy, buckwheat pancakes, sausage, bagels, filled doughnuts, and rolls.

The evening has a party atmosphere. The time has arrived for *shchedrivky*, the New Year's carols of good wishes for all. There may be fortune-telling, playful skits, and dressing in costume. In cities across the United States and Canada, restaurants and community groups host large and lively Malanka events, complete with traditional foods, Ukrainian music, and dancing, which during Soviet rule was prohibited during the Christmas season in Ukraine.

The next morning, be it St. Basil's feast day or the Feast of Jordan, the New Year is celebrated. What happens this day is important, for, according to an old Ukrainian saying, "As goes the New Year's Day, so goes the year." All are eager to set the best possible precedent for the coming year.

In Ukraine, and in some Ukrainian communities in the United States and Canada, boys go from house to house on this first day of the new year to sing shchedrivky, recite verses filled with good wishes, and scatter grains of wheat and other seeds on the floor of each home to "sow" prosperity and good luck in the year ahead.

During the years of Soviet domination, Grandfather Frost was introduced to Ukraine as a non-Christian replacement for St. Nicholas. Also, the Christmas tree and gift-giving traditions associated with St. Nicholas Day were moved to New Year's Day. For many Ukrainians raised during the Soviet years, the tree and gift-giving continue to be part of the New Year's celebration.

Christmas tree traditions

A lovingly decorated yalynka, or Christmas tree, can be seen in Ukrainian homes everywhere at Christmastime—if you know when

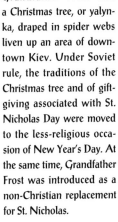

Grandfather Frost and a Christmas tree, or yalynka, draped in spider webs liven up an area of downtown Kiev. Under Soviet rule, the traditions of the Christmas tree and of gift-giving associated with St. Nicholas Day were moved to the less-religious occasion of New Year's Day. At the same time, Grandfather Frost was introduced as a non-Christian replacement for St. Nicholas.

to look. In some regions of Ukraine, particularly areas that may have been influenced by Christmas tree-loving German neighbors, the yalynka was a long-standing tradition. In other regions, the decorated Christmas tree was introduced by celebrating American G.I.'s during World War II.

However it came, the yalynka was a charming natural addition to St. Nicholas Day, the day for exchanging presents and receiving gifts from St. Nicholas himself. Traditionally, Ukrainian trees were likely to feature handcrafted ornaments, colored paper or foil, paper chains, sugar or honey cookies, polished apples, foil-covered nuts, and brightly wrapped candies. Straw ornaments shaped as stars or spiders and their webs were a natural addition to the Ukrainian tree. Tiny candles in special holders provided the light.

In cozy village cottages nestled in the snow, Ukrainian children also would sometimes create lovely Christmas decorations by sticking pieces of straw to a frosty windowpane.

When the Soviet Union dominated Ukraine, the Christmas tree and gift-giving traditions were officially moved to the less religious occasion of New Year's Day. Many Ukrainians raised during that long period of oppression continue to welcome their tree on this day. Other Ukrainians decorate their tree in time for Christmas morning, falling in step with their neighbors in countries around the world.

As Ukrainians revive their spirits in the new independence of their country, many are rediscovering the joy of traditions like St. Nicholas Day. And they are bringing back their own way of celebrating and their own perfect day for decorating a tree.

The Feast of Jordan

On this day, Orthodox priests bless the water that will be used to bless people, homes, and animals as the New Year begins. In the countryside, the blessing of the water takes place alongside a river. For this ceremony, the young men of the vil-

As part of the observance of the Feast of Jordan, Orthodox priests bless the water that will be used to bless people, homes, and animals for the New Year. In rural areas, the blessing takes place alongside a river, where young men construct a cross from blocks of ice cut from the frozen river. The cross may be stained red using beet *kvas* (a fermented infusion of beets).

Malanka

After so many years of Soviet oppression, it is no wonder that Ukrainians take their celebration of Christmas very seriously. At last these deeply religious people can practice their faith openly. And while many observances at this time of year are filled with religious reflection, there is one holiday that is pure fun—Malanka. Few cultures welcome the New Year with as much revelry as the people of Ukraine.

Many Malanka traditions are rooted in ancient pre-Christian rituals—in beliefs about good and evil spirits, and the conviction that good fortune in the new year is dependent on the enactment of certain rituals. In years past, Malanka was for men and boys only. But today women also participate in the festivities.

Malanka festivities resemble a Mardi Gras celebration—revelers of all shapes and sizes take to the streets for fun, excitement, and a little bit of mischief. By tradition, all must be masked for the entire festival. Often, participants choose masks that represent either good or evil spirits. Costumes come in all varieties. But always there is one young man dressed as a young girl, and this is the *MALANKA*, the character for whom the festivities are named. Surrounded by a company of revelers, the malanka leads the procession down the streets of the village.

Along their route participants stop at homes to sing carols; perform the vertep, or nativity; and offer good luck to the home, the family, and the harvest in the year to come. The malanka tries to do household chores, but does everything backward,

AND INEPTLY AT THAT. THIS CAUSES GREAT MERRIMENT.

SOME REVELERS SIT HIGH ATOP A TREE OUTSIDE THE HOME IN AN EFFORT TO CHASE AWAY ANY EVIL SPIRITS WHO MIGHT DARE TO SETTLE THERE. IN RETURN, THE PERFORMERS RECEIVE MONEY OR GOOD THINGS TO EAT.

IN SOME AREAS OF UKRAINE, THE MALANKA PROCESSION ENDS AT A FIELD WHERE COMPETITIONS TAKE PLACE. MANY OF THE CONTESTS PIT EVIL AGAINST GOOD. WHEN GOOD WINS, THERE WILL BE GOOD FORTUNE IN THE NEW YEAR.

AS IS THE CASE WITH ALL TRADITIONAL UKRAINIAN HOLIDAYS, THIS FEAST IS A BLEND OF THE PRE-CHRISTIAN AND AGRARIAN RITUALS COMBINED WITH THE NEWER CHRISTIAN THEMES. MALANKA ALSO ADDS A TOUCH OF FOLK THEATER.

AS MALANKA COMES TO A CLOSE, ALL HAVE HAD A GREAT TIME. AND AFTER ALL THE RITUALS OF ENSURING GOOD FORTUNE IN THE NEW YEAR HAVE BEEN PERFORMED, THE NEW YEAR ARRIVES, AND ONLY TIME WILL TELL IF WHAT HAS BEEN PREDICTED WILL TRULY COME TO PASS.

Parishioners celebrate the Feast of Jordan at a sunrise service on the river. Most have come with a container in hand to carry some of the blessed water back to their homes. There they will sprinkle the water on family members, about their homes, and on their farm animals to help ensure good fortune in the coming year.

lage construct a tall cross from blocks of ice cut from the river. The cross may be stained deep red using beet *kvas*.

In urban areas, large tubs of water are brought to the churches to be blessed and passed out to the worshipers. Today in Ukraine, the blessing of water is performed by priests in city squares as well as in churches.

Leaving the ceremony, parishioners take some of the blessed water to sprinkle on their families, all about their homes, and on their cattle. Family members also may drink some of the holy water and, after din-

ner, young girls may wash their face with it. In the past, it was customary for the village priest to visit every single home in the parish to perform the blessing ritual.

After a celebratory meal, the family's *yalynka*, or Christmas tree, is taken down and removed from the house. The didukh is then ceremonially burned. In the past, the hospodar would lead the family's cattle through the smoke of the burning didukh to give them protection from disease in the year ahead. Children might also leap high over the didukh's flames, hoping the spirits of their ancestors would not stay with them or cause bad luck in the year to come. The smoke was said to protect the fruit trees in the orchard and help bring a good harvest. On this occasion, farmers might also threaten unproductive trees with an ax or even give them a little hack, spurring them on to bear more fruit in the ensuing year.

On the morning of the next day, the Feast of St. John the Baptist, the kolaches that have been at the center of the table during the Christmas season are taken out and fed to the farm animals.

With these closing rites completed, the holiday period is ended and a new period for marriages is open until the beginning of Lent.

Homemade crosses decorate a well to bless the water contained within.

SONGS OF THE SEASON

Ukrainian Christmas carols, bearing the good tidings of Christmas and best wishes for the year ahead, embody the rich history of centuries of Christmas—and pre-Christmas—celebration in Ukraine.

With complex lyrics and ancient melodies particular to the Ukrainian tradition, these wonderful carols and the choirs that perform them have become a sacred sound of Christmas for people around the world. Who can resist the hauntingly beautiful "Carol of the Bells," which takes its music from a Ukrainian New Year's carol "Shchedryk, Shchedryk, Shchedrivochka"? And what better way to hear such music than performed at Christmas by one of the many world-class Ukrainian choirs?

Singing has always been a special part of the holiday season in Ukraine. In many American- and Canadian-Ukrainian churches, it is traditional that services from Christmas Day to the Feast of Jordan begin and end with the familiar carol "Boh Predvichnyi." Ukrainians claim that this Christmas carol has been sung by generation after generation longer than any other carol still in existence.

Since ancient times, Ukrainians have caroled to their friends and neighbors during the winter-cycle celebration of Koliada. The wealth and variety of traditional Ukrainian Christmas carols tell the story of Ukrainian Christmas celebrations past and present.

There are two types of Ukrainian carols: koliadky (carols sung at Christmastime) and shchedrivky (traditional New Year's songs). New types of koli-adky and shchedrivky have been added over the centuries to reflect the changing Ukraine.

Koliadky

Carols sung at Christmas are koliadky. The oldest of these carols, dating back to prehistory, address the creation of the universe. There are koliadky about the first birds, animals, people, and the forces of nature. Next come carols from the medieval era, many of which name specific people to be honored in their verse or retell historic events. More recently, carols were created describing aspects of daily life and the basic dreams and hopes of the individual. Koliada is also an ancient mythological figure of the winter ritual.

Finally, with the arrival of Christianity in Ukraine, new koli-adky were written about the birth of Jesus and about other religious themes. In addition, many of the older pre-Christian songs were "updated" with the addition of phrases referring to God or Jesus. Every Ukrainian child knows *"Dobryj Vechir Tobi, Pane Hospodarju"* ("Good Evening, Lord of This Household"). Sung each Christmas in Ukrainian homes around the world, this Christmas song is an ancient koliadka celebrating the winter festival of Koliada, to which the words "Rejoice, world, The Son of God is born," have been added as a refrain.

Shchedrivky

Shchedrivky, the other Ukrainian carols, are traditional New Year's songs. In some Ukrainian communities these songs offering good fortune in the coming year are sung at Shchedryi Vechir, or Generous Eve. Others wait until the Feast of Jordan. Looking to the spring ahead, shchedrivky celebrate the rebirth of nature. Shchedrivky offer wishes for fertile fields, healthy herds, and family prosperity in the new year. Many shchedrivky, like the well-loved "Carol of the Bells," mention the return of the swallows as a symbol of the spring season to come.

The central element of both koliadky and shchedrivky is their wish-come-true power. Whether describing great beauty, wealth, prosperity, wisdom, or love, carolers are offering the magic of their spoken wish to make good things happen.

Ukrainian carols are loved for their joyful and festive quality as well as their lovely melodies. In addition, their verse is noted for its poetic quality. Some of the best-known Ukrainian carols include *"Oi, vydyt Boh"* ("Oh, God Does See"), *"Boh predvichnyi"* ("The Eternal God"), *"Nova radist stala"* ("A New Joy Has Come"), *"V poli, poli pluzhok ore"* ("In the Field the Plow Is Plowing") and *"Nebo i zemlia"* ("Heaven and Earth").

Singing good wishes

Christmas in Ukraine is first a family holiday, shared in the close circle of family—past, present, and future—through age-old traditions. Yet, the warm glow of celebration quickly reaches beyond the home to friends, neighbors, and the world at large, as Ukrainian carolers and choirs brighten the winter days and nights with their beautiful offerings of Christmas cheer and good wishes.

The first koliadka is sung at the start of the Sviata Vecheria celebration. When the meal is finished, a koliadka is sung to the table in thanks for the meal. The spirited carol singing that began around the cozy family table continues on the way to midnight church services that night.

Some *koliadnyky*, or carolers, begin their rounds on Christmas Eve, but generally Christmas Day

> **Ukrainian carols are loved for their joyful and festive quality as well as their lovely melodies. In addition, their verse is noted for its poetic quality.**

opens the official caroling season. Early Christmas morning, young children hurry from house to house, offering a Christmas greeting and looking for holiday treats in return. Next, family members set out together for the homes of family and friends to share their Christmas joy in song. After the visitors "perform," everyone joins the singing. Then there is plenty of good food to enjoy.

By tradition, all carolers follow behind an 8- or 10-pointed star held high on a pole. The star, representing the Star of Bethlehem, is lit by a candle within and often has a nativity scene illustra-tion at its center. The group selects a *bereza*, or leader, to speak for them at each home.

First the bereza asks a hospodar, "Good folk, may we carol for you?" He is certain to be answered with a hearty, "*Prosymo!*" ("Please do!") After all, in their cheerful songs the carolers bring health, wealth, and beauty in for the year ahead.

According to ancient Ukrainian belief, the spoken word has the power to make things come true. When carolers sing to the hospodar that his crops will be abundant or sing to the daughter of the house that she is obedient and beautiful, they are not observing facts, but singing wishes so they will become facts in the year ahead. The home and every person in it is addressed with his or her own special song, following traditional songs for husbands, wives, children, daughters-in-law, sons-in-law, widows, priests and their families, grandparents, farm animals, and so on.

If a death has occurred in the family in the past year, a special koliadka for the dead is sung in his or her honor. Many koliadky address romantic themes, offering wish-fulfilling prophecies about love, matchmaking, and weddings to come.

After the traditional wishes

A Ukrainian bandura player performs koliadky.

are bestowed, the carolers are joined in joyful song by everyone present. The preholiday fast has been broken by the arrival of Christmas, so the carolers are rewarded for their singing with sumptuous food, rich pastries, and seasonal drinks. Carolers with many stops on their route may simply hold out a sack to receive nuts, fruits, candies, and other treats, plus a donation for a church or holiday charity they support. With a final carol of good wishes, they are off into the night.

The makeup of the caroling group varies by region or community. In eastern Ukraine, children and young people are usually the carolers. In the Hutsul region of the Carpathian Mountains in Western Ukraine, special groups of men, called *tabory*, are the traditional carolers. Here, each man carries an ax hung with Christmas bells on his shoulder. The group is led by a man carrying a cross. The group performs a small hopping dance and sings special dance songs, called *pliasaky*. After bowing three times to a house, they stop dancing. When the group leader sings a carol, the others join for the refrain of "Oi *dai Bozhe*" ("Oh, God, Grant It"), while ringing their bells and stomping their feet.

The men are invited in by the head of the house, while his wife ties a strand of flax around the cross. Once inside, these koliadnyky often perform humorous koliadky to "cheer up the household" before singing to each person present. The carolers receive

presents, then head out again to sing and dance elsewhere.

In addition to the star, Ukrainian caroling groups may carry aloft a *vertep*, or three-dimensional nativity scene, reenacting a tradition that dates back as far as the 1600's. Generally, the vertep is small and contained in a box atop a pole, though the nativity scene may be nearly life-size and require several men to carry it.

Some of the carolers in these groups dress as shepherds, wise men, and angels and, at each stop, present a Christmas play along with their carols. During Ukraine's long history of oppression, these Christmastime plays became an outlet for social commentary. Carolers dressed as soldiers, a Cossack, a grandmother, a gypsy, a courting couple, a nobleman, or a village elder were bound to draw rousing support for their clever comedies mocking all-too-familiar injustices. The practice of presenting these satirical skits was nearly extinguished

In some areas of Ukraine, the members of caroling groups dress as shepherds, wise men, and angels and perform a Christmas play. This tradition, long forbidden under Soviet rule, is making a strong comeback.

Ukrainian Choirs

FORTUNATELY, YOU DON'T HAVE TO BE A CLOSE NEIGHBOR TO HEAR UKRAINIAN CAROLS. UKRAINIANS LOVE TO SING. THEY SAY WHEREVER THERE ARE THREE UKRAINIANS IN ONE PLACE, YOU HAVE A CHOIR. HAPPILY, THIS SEEMS TO BE TRUE. UKRAINIAN CHOIRS, FAMOUS FOR THEIR BEAUTIFUL A CAPPELLA SINGING, HAVE FORMED WHEREVER UKRAINIANS SETTLED AROUND THE WORLD, AND THEY DRAW LARGE AUDIENCES WHENEVER THEY PERFORM. WORLD-CLASS CHOIRS, SUCH AS THE DUMKA CHOIR OF NEW YORK OR THE BANDURISTS CHOIR OF DETROIT, TOUR THE WORLD, ENTERTAINING SELL-OUT CROWDS.

AT CHRISTMAS, THESE CHOIRS OFFER A MIX OF STANDARD ENGLISH-LANGUAGE CAROLS WITH AN ASSORTMENT FROM THE BEAUTIFUL STOREHOUSE OF UKRAINIAN KOLIADKY AND SHCHEDRIVKY.

"CAROL OF THE BELLS," A CHRISTMAS CAROL LOVED AROUND THE WORLD, IS ACTUALLY AN ENGLISH ADAPTATION OF A UKRAINIAN SHCHEDRIVKA. A COMPARISON OF THE TWO VERSIONS' VERSES REVEALS THE LAYERS OF CELEBRATION INCLUDED IN MANY UKRAINIAN SONGS OF THE SEASON.

SHCHEDRYK

Shchedryk, shchedryk, shchedrivochka
A swallow flew in
And started to sing
Calling out the head of the house
"Come out, come out, head of the house,
Come look on your homestead

Over there the ewes have rolled
And the lambs are newly born
Your animals are all well fed

You will receive much money."
Your wife is good looking
If you get no money, then you'll have chaff
But your wife is good looking."
Shchedryk, shchedryk, shchedrivochka
A swallow flew in
And started to sing (Repeats)

IN 1919, AMERICANS ADOPTED A NEW CHRISTMAS FAVORITE WHEN THE UKRAINIAN REPUBLICAN CAPELLA CHOIR ON A NORTH AMERICAN TOUR SANG THE UKRAINIAN SHCHEDRIVKA WITH NEW ENGLISH WORDS.

CAROL OF THE BELLS

Hark to the bells, hark to the bells,
Telling us all Jesus is King!
Strongly they chime, sound with a rhyme,
Christmas is here! Welcome the King.
Hark to the bells, Hark to the bells,
This is the day, day of the King!

under repressive Soviet rule and is only now being revived in some areas of Ukraine.

In times past, winter cycle carolers were accompanied by a boy costumed as a goat, the *koza*. At each house, the koza would bow to the family, then perform a ritual dance to help ensure a good harvest while the other carolers sang "Where the Goat goes, there wheat grows; where the Goat stamps his feet, there are seven sheaves of wheat." On leaving, the goat delivered his spoken wish, "May this farmer's cattle be unbedeviled and full of milk and may his oats sow themselves and his wheat be of the best sort." As Christianity took hold, the goat became more of an amusement for children.

The koza, or goat, performs for the amusement of Ukrainian youngsters. This costumed character is a holdover from the ancient Ukrainian celebration of the winter cycle.

UKRAINIAN CRAFTS

Didukh

The didukh is used to commemorate a family's ancestors. A didukh floor decoration can range from 3 to 6 feet tall. The directions given here enable you to make a didukh that stands approximately 19 inches tall and can be used as a centerpiece or hung on a wall.

Materials

- wheat stalks (50 or more, depending on desired width of didukh), found in craft stores
- 24-gauge florist wire (found in craft stores)
- scissors
- wide ribbon (1 yard of 1½"-wide ribbon for small bundle)
- dried flowers (optional)

What to Do

1. Gather wheat stalks into a bunch.

2. Holding the bunch in one hand, wrap florist wire 6 to 8 times around stalks, approximately ⅓ of the way down from the wheat tops.

3. After bunch is tightly wound, leave five inches of wire unwrapped and cut wire with scissors. Push cut wire end under wrapped wires on stalk and pull tightly to secure (figure 1). Bend wire end into a loop, and twist to form hanger (figure 2).

Figure 1.   Figure 2.

4. Using scissors, trim bottoms of wheat stalks to the same length.

5. Using the ribbon, tie a bow around the stalks. Ribbon should cover the wrapped wire but not the hanger.

6. Dried flowers may be tucked under the ribbon.

Spider Ornament

Read a Ukrainian tale about a Christmas spider on page 22. Then make this adorable spider ornament to hang on your tree or perch on the edge of a platter as a table decoration.

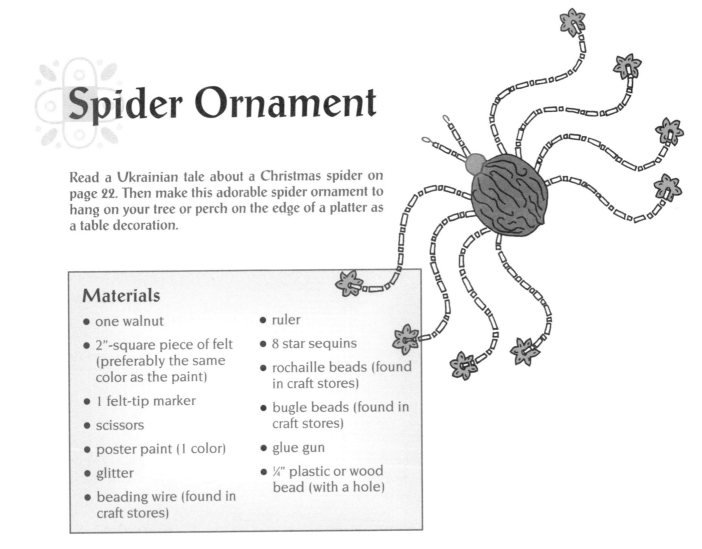

Materials

- one walnut
- 2"-square piece of felt (preferably the same color as the paint)
- 1 felt-tip marker
- scissors
- poster paint (1 color)
- glitter
- beading wire (found in craft stores)
- ruler
- 8 star sequins
- rochaille beads (found in craft stores)
- bugle beads (found in craft stores)
- glue gun
- ¼" plastic or wood bead (with a hole)

What to Do

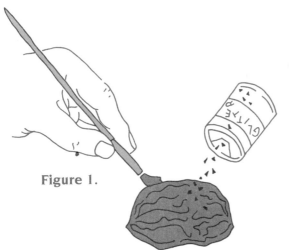

Figure 1.

1 Pry apart a walnut shell into 2 equal halves. Carefully remove and discard nut meat from one half. Set aside remaining half for another use.

2 Place shell half on felt, cavity side down. With marker, trace bottom of shell onto felt. Cut out and set aside.

3 Paint outside of shell half and sprinkle with glitter before paint dries to secure glitter to shell (figure 1). Set aside to dry.

4 With scissors, cut eight 5" pieces of beading wire (figure 2).

Cut eight 5" pieces of wire

Figure 2.

5 Take one cut wire and start beading by first pushing a star sequin through the wire until ¼" of wire extends beyond the sequin. Bend the ¼" of wire behind the sequin to secure (figure 3). Repeat with the remaining 7 wires.

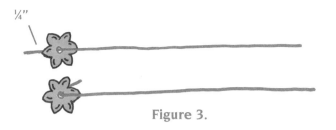

¼"

Figure 3.

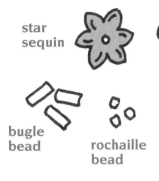

star sequin

bugle bead

rochaille bead

6 Starting with a rochaille bead, alternately thread 1 rochaille bead, then 1 bugle bead, until only 1" of wire remains. Bend the remaining wire to form a loop (figure 4). You have now formed a beaded wire leg for the spider. Repeat with remaining 7 wires.

Figure 4.

bent wire loop

7 Turn over shell to expose the inside cavity. Using a marker, draw 8 dots on shell edge (4 per side) as a guide for placement of the beaded wire legs. With the looped end of the beaded wire leg facing in toward cavity, bend the loop inside the cavity (figure 5). Use a generous amount of hot glue to secure looped wire in place. Hold in place until glue is set. Repeat this process until all 8 wires are in place.

8 When the glue for all the wires has set and the wires are secure, place some glue around perimeter of shell edge and attach previously cut felt piece (direction #2) to shell bottom. This will give a finished look to the spider as well as hide the wires.

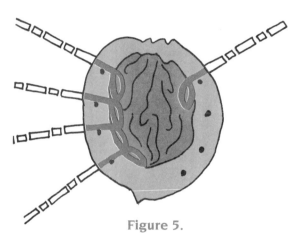

Figure 5.

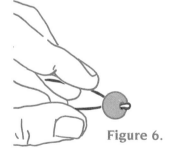

Figure 6.

9 To form the head of the spider, start by cutting one 2" piece of wire with scissors. Bend the cut wire in half. Push the two loose wire ends through a ¼" plastic bead hole until only a small loop is protruding (figure 6). Bend small loop back toward bead.

10 Push beads onto the two loose wire ends. Starting with a rochaille bead, alternate with a bugle bead until you have threaded two of each kind of bead. Bend back remaining exposed wire into a loop to secure beads. With a glue gun, glue ¼" plastic bead to end of walnut, centering between the two groups of four beaded wire legs.

11 Bend the beaded wires up and down in a wavy fashion to complete spider.

12 Nestle spider on a tree branch, or wrap one wire leg around branch to secure ornament to tree. Or, use as a table decoration.

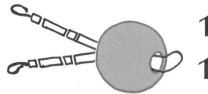

Figure 7.

Dough Ornament

Craft this small wreath to hang on the tree as an ornament, or place a paper doily beneath it on a plate and lay flat as a table decoration.

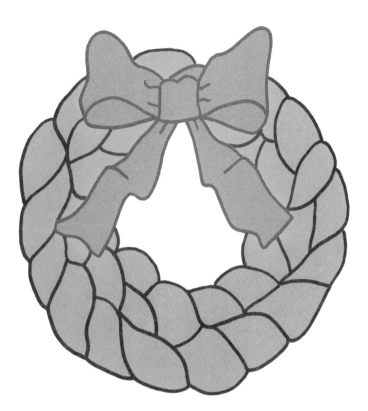

Materials

- ½ cup flour
- ¼ cup salt
- ¼ cup water
- mixing bowl
- spoon
- butter knife
- baking sheet
- nonstick cooking spray
- spatula
- polyurethane spray varnish (optional)
- ribbon (¼" wide and 16" long)
- 24-gauge florist wire (found in craft stores)
- dried flowers, rose hip berries, wheat stalk tops (optional)

What to Do

1 First, make the dough.* To do so, combine flour, salt, and water in a mixing bowl and mix to form a pliable dough. Add more water (one teaspoon at a time) if necessary. Knead for 10 minutes.

2 Place dough on work surface. With a butter knife, divide dough into six equal parts.

3 Roll each dough piece by hand into a 9" rope, about ¼" thick (figure 1). If dough is sticking to work surface, sprinkle surface with a small amount of flour and continue rolling.

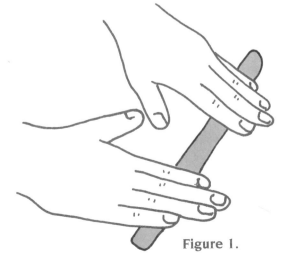

Figure 1.

* Dough is not edible.

4 Using two ropes at a time, twist the pieces together (figure 2). Repeat with the remaining 4 ropes.

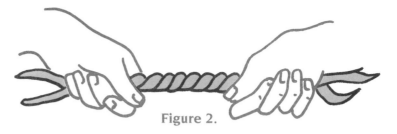

Figure 2.

5 Braid the 3 twisted ropes together (figure 3).

6 Connect the ends of the braid to form a circle approximately 4" in diameter. Seal the ends closed by pinching them together. If dough ends do not adhere easily, moisten ends with a small amount of water before pinching closed.

7 Spray a baking sheet with nonstick cooking spray, place dough wreath on baking sheet, and bake in a low-temperature oven (225 °F) until thoroughly dry—approximately 4-6 hours.

8 When braid is baked, remove from baking sheet with a spatula. Let cool.

9 To protect dough wreath and to obtain a golden-brown color, you may spray with varnish on a well-protected work surface.

Figure 3.

10 When the wreath is thoroughly dried, decorate it by making a bow out of ribbon. Attach the bow to the wreath by pushing florist wire through knot at back of bow (figure 4) and wrapping wire around braid. Twist the ends of the wire together to close. This will also serve as a hanger.

11 Additional decorations may be added. Dried flowers, rose hip berries, and wheat stalks may be tucked behind bow. (Keep the decorations small in scale to match wreath proportion.)

florist wire

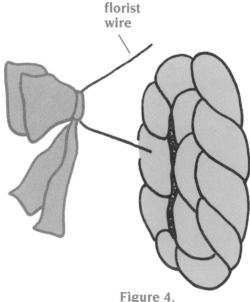

Figure 4.

Bookmarks

Inspired by the intricately beautiful designs found on Ukrainian eggs and wooden inlay boxes, these bookmarks are great gifts for children to make.

Materials

- pencil
- ruler
- construction paper of assorted colors
- scissors
- glue
- paper hole punch
- ready-made tassel (found in craft stores)

What to Do

1 With a pencil and ruler, measure and draw a 2¼" x 7" rectangle on a piece of construction paper. Cut out the rectangle using the scissors. Set it aside.

2 Cut many rectangles, squares, triangles, and circles out of the construction paper. Use a variety of colors.

3 Place the small cut-out shapes on the 2¼" x 7" rectangle. Position the shapes to form a pattern. You may use one of the patterns on the next page or make up your own. Remember to leave ¾" of space at the top of the large background rectangle for the tassel.

4 When you are happy with your design, glue each piece down. Let the glue dry before you begin the next step.

5 In the blank area you left at the top of the bookmark, place a pencil mark centered both vertically and horizontally. With the paper hole punch, punch a hole for the tassel where this pencil mark is.

6 Tie a tassel in the punched hole.

7 For durability, the bookmark may also be laminated before the hole is punched and tassel attached. (Many office supply and stationery stores laminate.)

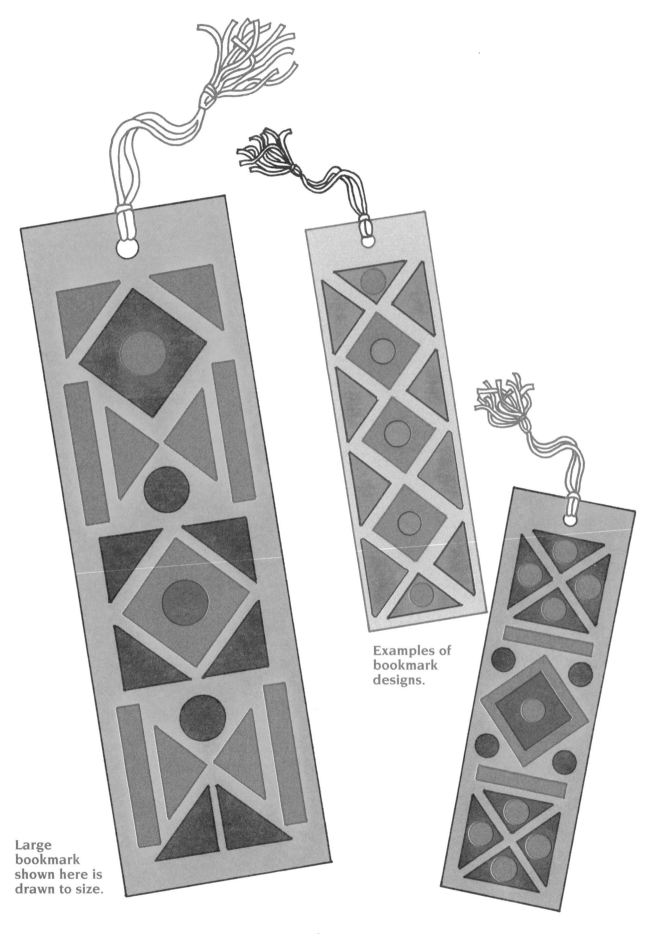

Examples of
bookmark
designs.

Large
bookmark
shown here is
drawn to size.

UKRAINIAN CAROLS

Eternal God

1. E - ter - nal God this day — was born.

Com - ing — down from a - bove to re -

deem us with His love, Christ, the Son of God.

2. In Bethlehem
   to us was born
   Savior, King,
   Sov'reign Lord,
   the Messiah of our world,
   Christ, the Son of God.

3. Let us exclaim:
   "Glory to God!"
   Homage we give
   to God's Son,
   honoring the Blessed One
   Christ, the Son of God.

All the Universe Rejoices

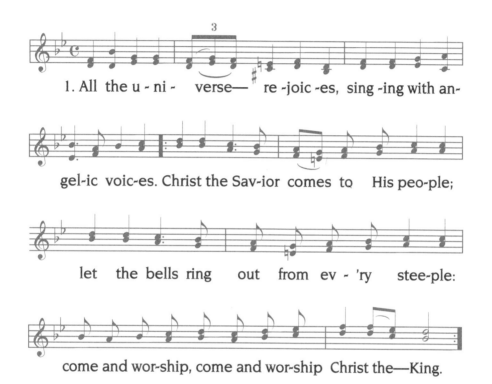

1. All the u - ni - verse— re -joic -es, sing -ing with an-
gel-ic voic-es. Christ the Sav-ior comes to His peo-ple;
let the bells ring out from ev - 'ry stee-ple:
come and wor-ship, come and wor-ship Christ the—King.

2. Three wise men brought from
   their dominions
   gifts of gold and myrrh and incense
   To the Master of all creation;
   join them in this holy celebration:
   come and worship,
   come and worship
   Christ the King.

Heaven and Earth

1. Heav-en and earth, heav-en and earth now wel-come their Re-deem-er.

An-gels and peo - ple, an-gels and peo - ple join in a cel - e -

bra — tion Je-sus Christ is born— on this bless-ed morn;

angel choirs are singing; wise men gifts are bringing; shepherds tell the sto-ry;

star pro-claims the glo - ry; for the Sav-ior of the world is born.

2. In Bethlehem, in Bethlehem
   God's Word is given birth,
   born of a virgin, born of a virgin,
   Master of heaven and the earth.
   Jesus Christ is born on this
     blessed morn;
   angels choirs are singing;
   wise men gifts are bringing;
   shepherds tell the story;
   star proclaims the glory;
   for the Savior of the world is born.

3. Come and adore Him,
     come and adore Him
   lying there in a manger.
   Lift up your voices,
     lift up your voices,
   singing praises to the Savior.
   Jesus Christ is born on this
     blessed morn;
   angels choirs are singing;
   wise men gifts are bringing;
   shepherds tell the story;
   star proclaims the glory;
   for the Savior of the world is born.

Borsch with Vushka
(Meatless Beet Soup with Mushroom Dumplings)

¼ lb. dried mushrooms
  (boletus or porcini)
1 medium onion, chopped
2 tbsp. olive oil
3 medium beets, cut into quarters
3 whole peppercorns
6 cups water

1 carrot, chopped
1 celery stalk, chopped
1 sprig parsley
1 tbsp. lemon juice or vinegar
salt and pepper (to taste)
1 tsp. dried dill
vushka (*recipe below*)

   Rinse mushrooms in hot water; drain well. Place mushrooms in a medium-sized saucepan, cover with water, and soak for 1 hour. Place saucepan over low heat and cook mushrooms in the same water until tender, about 1 to 2 hours. Remove mushrooms and set aside for vushka (*below*). Reserve the mushroom stock.

   Sauté onion in oil until golden. Add beets, peppercorns, and water. Cover and simmer over low heat until beets are crisp-tender. Add carrot, celery, and parsley and simmer another 15 minutes or until vegetables are tender. Add lemon juice or vinegar; mix well. Add reserved mushroom stock, salt, pepper, and dill. Add prepared vushka.

   Serves 8 to 10.

Vushka (Mushroom Dumplings)

mushrooms from borsch (*above*)
3 six-oz. jars whole mushrooms, drained
2 medium onions, chopped

2 tbsp. butter
salt and pepper (to taste)
plain breadcrumbs, if necessary

   Combine mushrooms in a medium saucepan. Cover with water, bring to a boil, reduce heat, and then simmer for 1 hour. Strain liquid; discard. Grind mushrooms in a meat grinder or food processor three or four times.

   Sauté onions in butter until transparent. Add mushrooms and salt and pepper to taste. If there is too much liquid, add plain breadcrumbs to soak up the excess.

   For the dough, use the recipe for pyrohy dough on page 76. Roll dough out to ⅛-inch thickness. Using a butter knife, cut out 2-inch squares of dough.

   Place 1 teaspoon of filling in the center of each square. Fold diagonally to make a triangle. Press edges together to seal. Bring together the two bottom corners of the triangle, and seal. Bring a large pot of salted water to a boil. Drop vushka one by one into boiling water; cook until they float to the top. Remove with a slotted spoon, drain, and serve in borsch.

Pyrohy (Stuffed Dumplings)

5 cups flour
1 tsp. salt
1 stick margarine, softened

3 eggs
1½ cups water
Potato and Cheese Filling (*recipe below*)

Mix flour and salt on a breadboard or in a wide bowl. Make a well in the center of the mixture and add eggs, margarine, and ¼ cup water. Mix well and knead lightly to make a smooth dough. If dough is too dry, add more water, 1 tablespoon at a time, until dough is smooth and elastic. Cover and let sit in a warm place for 10 to 15 minutes. Prepare Potato and Cheese Filling. Refrigerate until needed.

Divide dough into three equal parts. On a floured surface, roll one part of the dough to ⅛-inch thickness. Cut 3-inch rounds with a large biscuit cutter or drinking glass. Place one tablespoon of filling to one side of each round, moisten one edge, then press edges together firmly to seal. Place filled pyrohy on floured surface and cover while preparing the remaining pyrohy. Repeat with remaining dough. Bring a wide pot of water to a boil. Drop 8 to 10 pyrohy in the boiling water. Cook gently for 3 to 4 minutes or until pyrohy float to the surface. Lift out with a slotted spoon. Place on a lightly greased plate or toss gently with melted butter.

Potato and Cheese Filling for Pyrohy

6 medium white potatoes
2 medium onions, chopped
2 tbsp. butter

8 oz. American cheese, grated
1 cup dry curd cottage cheese
salt and pepper

Boil potatoes in their skins until tender. Cool, peel, and mash. Melt butter in a large skillet. Sauté onions in butter until golden. Combine cheeses, onions, and potatoes in a large bowl. Season with salt and pepper to taste. Use for filling in prepared pyrohy dough (*see recipe above*).

Uzvar (Dried Fruit Compote)

Prepare this dish ahead of time to allow the flavors to blend.

2 lbs. mixed dried fruit (apples,
    pears, prunes, apricots, raisins)

16 cups water
1½ cups honey

Place dried fruit in a large saucepan. Add water and honey. Cover the pan and simmer the fruit mixture until fruit is soft. Add more water, if necessary. Allow compote to cool, then taste for sweetness.
Serves 10-12.

Medivnyk (Honey Cake)

½ cup butter
1 cup sugar
4 eggs, separated
1 cup honey
1 cup sour cream
3 cups flour, sifted
2 tsp. baking soda

2 tsp. baking powder
1 tsp. cinnamon
½ tsp. ground nutmeg
¼ tsp. salt
1 cup raisins
1 cup walnuts, chopped

Preheat oven to 300 °F. In a large bowl, cream butter and sugar until light. Add egg yolks one at a time, beating well after each addition. Add honey and sour cream alternately, mixing well.

Beat egg whites until stiff. Sift together the flour, baking soda, baking powder, cinnamon, nutmeg, and salt. Fold the flour mixture alternately with the egg whites into the batter. Fold in the raisins and walnuts. Pour batter into two well-greased and floured loaf pans. Bake 1 hour or until a toothpick inserted into the cake comes out clean. Remove cakes from pans; place on a wire rack to cool.

Serves 10 to 12.

Christmas Honey Balls

1 stick margarine
4 cups flour
1 cup honey
1 cup sour cream

4 eggs
2 tsp. baking soda
2 tsp. baking powder
48 walnut halves

Preheat oven to 350 °F. Cut margarine into flour with a pastry knife. Place honey in a microwave-safe bowl and heat on 50% power until bubbling. (Alternatively, place honey in a heat-resistant glass cup and place cup in a pan of hot water; stir.) Add honey to flour and margarine; stir well. Add sour cream, eggs, baking soda, and baking powder. Knead into a smooth dough. Add more flour, 1 tablespoon at a time, until dough is no longer sticky.

Pinch off small pieces of dough and roll into ¾-inch balls. Place balls on greased cookie sheet. Press a walnut half into the center of each cookie. Bake for 15 to 20 minutes, until golden. Cool on a wire rack.

Makes 48 cookies.

Holubtsi (Stuffed Cabbage)

2 cups rice, uncooked
1 large head white cabbage
1 large onion, chopped
2 tbsp. butter

Mushroom Filling (*recipe below*)
salt and pepper
Mushroom Sauce (*recipe below*)
½ cup sour cream

Prepare rice according to package directions. Remove core from cabbage. Place cabbage head in large pot of boiling water. Cover and cook for 3 minutes. Remove softened whole leaves from the cabbage head. Slice off part of the thick ribs on the leaves so that leaves are more pliable.

Prepare Mushroom Filling. Then, melt buter in a large skillet. Sauté onion in butter until transparent. Add mushroom filling and rice to onion. Line bottom of a casserole dish with cabbage leaves not suitable for stuffing. Fill stem part of each leaf with 2 to 3 heaping tablespoons of filling. Fold sides over and then roll leaf from bottom to top. Place seam side down in casserole dish. Cover with Mushroom Sauce, to which you have added ½ cup sour cream. Bake covered at 350 °F for 1 to 1½ hours.

Mushroom Filling for Holubtsi

¾ cup dried mushrooms
   (boletus or porcini)
3 six-oz. jars whole mushrooms, drained

2 tbsp. butter
2 medium onions, chopped
salt and pepper to taste

Place dried and bottled mushrooms in a medium saucepan. Cover with water and bring to a boil. Reduce heat and simmer for 1 to 2 hours. Strain liquid from mushrooms. Grind mushrooms in a meat grinder or food processor three or four times. Melt butter in a large skillet. Sauté onions in butter until transparent. Add mushrooms and salt and pepper to taste.

Mushroom Sauce for Roast Beef or Holubtsi

¼ cup chopped onions
2 tbsp. butter
1 cup chopped fresh mushrooms
1 tbsp. flour

½ cup beef or vegetable broth
1 tsp. chopped parsley
salt and pepper

Melt butter in a large skillet. Add onions and sauté until tender. Add mushrooms and cook for about 10 to 12 minutes. Sprinkle flour over mushroom mixture and stir well. Pour in broth and stir constantly until mixture thickens. Cook for a few more minutes. Remove from heat and stir in parsley. Season with salt and pepper to taste.

Walnut Torte

9 eggs, separated
¾ cup sugar
9 to 10 oz. finely ground walnuts (about 2 ¼ cups)
4 heaping tbsp. fine breadcrumbs
1 tsp. baking powder
1 tsp. vanilla
1 tbsp. brandy or sherry
Coffee Custard Filling (*recipe below*)
Frosting (*recipe below*)
candied violets (optional)
mint sprigs (optional)

Preheat oven to 350 °F. Beat 8 egg yolks until thick and lemon colored. Add sugar gradually, beating on high until mixture is thick. Fold in ground walnuts and breadcrumbs. Add baking powder. In a separate bowl, beat egg whites until stiff but not dry. Fold egg whites into walnut mixture. Add vanilla. Grease a 9- or 10-inch springform pan and dust with breadcrumbs. Spoon in batter. Bake 50 to 60 minutes. A toothpick will come out clean when done.

Cool for a few minutes. With a sharp knife, loosen edges of torte from sides of pan, remove gently from pan, and invert, keeping bottom of pan in place. Cool on a wire rack. When torte is cool, remove bottom of the pan with a knife and place torte on wax paper. Cut torte into 2 or 3 layers using a sharp knife. Sprinkle 2 bottom layers with brandy or sherry. Spread with Coffee Custard Filling and frost. Decorate with candied violets and mint sprigs, if desired.

Coffee Custard Filling for Walnut Torte

1½ sticks unsalted butter
½ cup sugar
2 tsp. instant coffee dissolved in 2 tbsp. boiling water
1 heaping tbsp. cocoa
1 snack-sized container (4 oz.) ready-to-eat vanilla pudding

Cream together butter and sugar until light and fluffy. Add remaining ingredients and mix until consistency is suitable for spreading.

Frosting for Walnut Torte

2 four-oz. bars German sweet baker's chocolate
6 tbsp. milk
2 tbsp. unsalted butter

Melt chocolate in a double boiler. Add milk and butter. Stir until creamy. Pour over the top of torte.

ACKNOWLEDGMENTS

Cover	© Tania D'Avignon
2	© T Resource from Tony Stone Images
5	ITAR-TASS from Sovfoto/Eastfoto
6	© Tania D'Avignon
9	ITAR-TASS from Sovfoto/Eastfoto
10	© Eric Lessing, Art Resource
13	© Tania D'Avignon
14	© Eugene G. Schulz, Schulz Global Travel
15	© Tania D'Avignon
16	© Jeffrey Sylvester, FPG
17-19	Dale DeBolt*
20-23	© Tania D'Avignon
24	Joann Seastrom*
25	© D. Mossienko, Trip Photographic Library
26	© Miro Vintoniv, The Picture Cube
29	© D. Mossienko, Trip Photographic Library
30	Holy Transfiguration Monastery/Ukrainian Research Institute/Harvard University
31	© Superstock
32-35	© D. Mossienko, Trip Photographic Library
37	© Tania D'Avignon
38	© Jacques Hnizdovsky/Ukrainian Research Institute/Harvard University
40	Sovfoto/Eastfoto
42-45	© D. Mossienko, Trip Photographic Library
46	© Tania D'Avignon
47	© D. Mossienko, Trip Photographic Library
48	© Serhiy Marchenko
50	© Frank S. Balthis, Nature's Design
51-55	© Tania D'Avignon
56	© Frank S. Balthis, Nature's Design
59	© D. Mossienko, Trip Photographic Library
60	Sovfoto/Eastfoto
61	© Tania D'Avignon
63	© Frank S. Balthis, Nature's Design
64	© D. Mossienko, Trip Photographic Library

Craft Illustrations:
    Nancy Moroney*

All entries marked with an asterisk (*) denote illustrations created exclusively for World Book, Inc.